"God Bless Chesty"

A first person account of the making of a Marine in

the year 1969

By G. W. Andrews

Copyright

Table of Contents

Forward

Chapter 1.   The Decision

Chapter 2.   The Processing Station

Chapter 3.   The Arrival

Chapter 4.   The First Night

Chapter 5.   Processing Days

Chapter 6.   First Phase Training

Chapter 7.   Medical Rehabilitation Platoon

Chapter 8.   Back to Training

Chapter 9.   The Rifle Range

Chapter 10.   Final Phase

Chapter 11.   Night before Graduation

Chapter 12.   Graduation

Chapter 13.   Camp Pendleton

Epilog

Acknowledgements

Forward

This book is the first person account of a young man going through Marine Corps boot camp in the year 1969. It is not intended to reflect how today's Marines are trained., although I suspect all Marines, past and present, will be able to relate to much of what is written here. The training was harsh in many respects, as it needed to be. We were, after all, training to go to war.

I have related my experiences in boot camp exactly as I recall them, changing only names other than my own. I have not exaggerated or embellished anything, nor have I softened anything. The language was as harsh as the men who trained us. We learned many "colorful" phrases while in training such as "fucking A" (Marine talk for "you bet your ass"), "bends and motherfuckers" (everyone's least favorite exercise), "Susie Rotten Crotch" (the girl back home), and a wide range of military words unfamiliar to us that were often preceded by some form of the word fuck.

While some may question the training methods employed in Marine Corps boot camp in that era, none can argue with the results. We reported to the recruit depot as scared, young, and undisciplined men. We stood at attention on graduation day as hardened, physically fit, mentally tough, and disciplined United States Marines. The transformation in just a few weeks' time was nothing short of miraculous. Not all made it through the training, but those that did swelled with pride on graduation day and every day after for the rest of their lives.

This book is dedicated to every person who has the courage to wear the eagle, globe, and anchor.......past, present, and future.

Chapter 1. The Decision

"Welcome to Marine Corps Recruit Depot San Diego." These were the first words spoken to us upon arrival for recruit training. What was to follow made us feel anything but welcome.

The year was 1969. It was an era of contradictions. The peace and free love movements were still going strong, hippies were getting high, rock and roll owned the airwaves, long hair was in, and respect for authority was at an all-time low. But against this backdrop, America also swelled with pride as Neil Armstrong walked on the moon. Computers and technology were starting to impact the way we did things. Americans were optimistic about the future of our country, but at the same time terribly divided over the war we found ourselves engaged in. Viet Nam had become a quagmire, with American lives being lost daily. Graphic war scenes were broadcast on the nightly news programs. As unpopular as the military draft was, it was still in effect and a major concern for every young man as he turned 18 years of age.

As for me, 1969 had been the best year I could have hoped for. It was my senior year of high school and it met all of my expectations. I lettered in football, basketball, and track. I had a steady girlfriend and attended all of the big dances, including the prom. These were all things that I aspired to as an underclassman and they all became a reality for me in my senior year. And in spite of giving little to no importance to my studies, I did manage to graduate. My father arranged a summer job for me at the company he was employed by, and I experienced my first taste of the "real" world. I learned that it was a place where it no longer mattered whether you played ball or not, whether you had a girlfriend or not, or whether you were popular or not. You needed to act in a responsible way and work hard. If you did, you were rewarded with a paycheck. There were no cheerleaders, no roaring crowds urging you on, no underclassmen treating you like you were a god of some sort. This was quite different from the world I had become accustomed to in high school, but I made the adjustment. I used my earnings over the summer to purchase a Jawa 90 motorcycle. It wasn't a large or powerful bike, but it was candy apple red and was just the coolest thing I had ever owned.

As the summer came to an end, the time had come to decide what I wanted to do with my life. My father had accepted a promotion in his company that required him and the rest of the family to make preparations for an overseas assignment. That meant that laying around on the couch and hoping my draft number didn't come up was not going to be an option for me. No, I had a big decision to make at the tender young age of 18.

As with all young men coming out of high school in those years, I had three basic options. I could seek full time work at a low skill entry-level position and hope my draft number didn't come up. Or I could enter college and apply for a draft deferment. Or I could choose to volunteer for military service and enlist. Working in a grocery store or gas station didn't appeal to me and those were the only types of jobs I saw that were hiring young men right out of high school, so option one was out. I was a jock in high school and was only concerned with keeping my grades high enough to remain eligible for varsity athletics. In spite of my lack of effort in scholastic pursuits, I had taken "college prep" courses and my grades would have been sufficient to get me into a number of colleges if I had chosen this option. Had I received any athletic scholarship offers, I may well have accepted one just so I could continue playing ball. But it was difficult to get noticed by college recruiters when you played for a brand new school which happened to be the doormat for the league in all sports. I had no interest in going to school for the educational benefit of it alone, so option two was out. That left option three, enlistment in the military.

Having settled on the enlistment option, the next step was to select which branch of the military I would prefer to serve in. I was being bombarded with literature from all branches through the mail, and I studied each and every mailing I received. My father had served in the Air Force, and I had a cousin on his side of the family that had attended the Air Force Academy and was serving as an officer. His younger brother, a cousin closer to my age, was in the process of enlisting in the Air Force as well, so there was a measure of family tradition connected to the Air Force. I initially gave this option a lot of consideration, but learned that since the Air Force was considered the "safest" of the branches during the Viet Nam era, there was a waiting list of young men trying to enlist in that particular branch. If I wanted to wear the Air Force blue, I would have to wait for an opening and hope my draft number didn't come up in the meantime. No, it would have to be another branch of the military. The other branch that had family tradition connected to it was the Marine Corps. An uncle on my mother's side had served as a Marine in World War II, and his son, my cousin, was currently in the Marine Corps and had served a tour of duty in Viet Nam. After briefly flirting with the idea of "seeing the world" in the Navy, and then deciding that shipboard life would not be my cup of tea, I looked hard at what the Marine Corps had to say in their mailings.

The Marines spoke of things like tradition, honor, and courage in their literature. This was terminology that appealed to me. The literature went on to point out that the Marine Corps was a small force in comparison to the "big three" and had high standards and even higher demands. They made no secret of the fact that their training was the toughest in the business and that not everyone was cut out to be a Marine. This also appealed to me because if I was to enter the military and quite possibly find myself in a war zone, I wanted to know that I had the best training available and that I was thoroughly prepared. I also wanted to know that the men I would be serving with were equally well trained and prepared, since on the field of battle my life may depend on the actions of those around me. I feared that if I opted for the Army instead, I would potentially be surrounded by draftees who were under trained and really didn't want to be there. The Marines challenged me by not asking me to join, but rather by asking "are you good enough" to be a Marine? I was in good physical condition from my athletic pursuits, and had developed a "hard nose" attitude playing football. I was confident I could pass a written exam and I was equally confident that I could handle the tough physical training. Was I good enough to be a Marine? Damn straight! I lived in the Riverside, California area and made plans to go downtown to see the Marine Corps recruiter.

The recruiting office in Riverside at that

time was a joint recruiting center with all the services located in the same building. I walked straight down the long hall past the Army, Navy, and Air Force offices without even glancing inside. I was a young man on a mission. I walked into the Marine Corps office and announced confidently to the smartly uniformed man sitting at the desk that I wanted to be a Marine. He carefully set his cup of coffee on the desk in front of him and looked me over with eyes that seemed to penetrate right through me and look directly into my soul.

"And what makes you think you are good enough to join my Marine Corps, son?" he asked in a firm tone of voice.

I had worn my lettermen's jacket in hopes of impressing the recruiter, who didn't seem to be all that impressed.

"I'm in shape, I'm smart, and I have family already in the Marines, so I'm ready to go," I replied in my most manly voice.

"Did you graduate from high school?" he asked.

"Yes I did," I offered. "I have my diploma, my birth certificate, and my social security card right here if you need to see them."

He collected my documents and left the room for a moment to make copies. I scanned the room as I waited for him to return, fascinated by the various recruiting posters adorning the walls. The more I saw of these Marines, the more I wanted to be one of them. When he returned to his desk, the recruiting sergeant handed my documents back to me and pulled out a screening test.

"I want you to sit over there at that table and complete this test," he directed. "If you do well enough on this one, we'll see about scheduling you for the real deal."

I grabbed a pencil and began working on the multiple choice questions in front of me. I had little trouble with the questions on the test and had it completed in short order. When the sergeant placed the answer key over it, I detected just a hint of a smile.

"Based on this test, I would say your chances of passing the entrance exam are excellent. How about health issues? Can you think of any reason you might not pass a physical?" he inquired.

"Nope. I'm in great shape physically," I

answered with confidence.

"And you understand that your country is at war, and if you join the Marines you may well see combat?" he asked in a very serious tone.

"I do understand that. And if that happens, I'd rather be trained by the Marines than by any other branch of service," I replied, doing my best to match the seriousness of his tone.

"Well then, it seems to me that you have thought this through carefully. It also appears that you may be the caliber of young man we are looking for. Would you like me to schedule you for the entrance exam and physical?"

"That's what I came for," I replied.

The next couple of hours were spent completing what seemed like hundreds of forms and watching as the recruiting sergeant struggled with the typewriter that was now the tool of his trade rather than a rifle. I'm sure he would have been more comfortable with a rifle in his hands instead of that old manual typewriter, as "hunt and peck" didn't even begin to describe the tortured process he was going through preparing my paperwork. Somehow, he got through it and presented me with a packet that I was to take to Los Angeles on the date he scheduled for me to test and physical. He also presented me with a bus ticket for my transportation and a voucher for the Los Angeles hotel I was to stay in the night before the test. I had a two week wait before my scheduled processing date.

"Any questions?" he asked.

"No questions," I replied. "I'm ready for this."

"I believe you are," offered the sergeant as he put his hand out and gave me the firmest handshake I had ever experienced in my young life. "I believe you are".

A wave of emotions coursed through me as I left the office and climbed aboard my Jawa 90 for the ride home. I felt enormous pride in the fact that the Marine Corps seemed to want me, and was excited about the prospect of wearing the Marine Corps uniform in the near future. The other branches of service had good looking uniforms too, but that Marine Corps dress blue uniform had no equal. At the same time, the "what have I done" syndrome also found its' way into the pit of my

21

stomach. What was boot camp really like? Was I tough enough to complete the training? What about afterwards? Where would I be stationed? Would I go to Viet Nam? Would I see combat? And then when I thought of how I would tell my parents what I had done, my stomach started turning flips and I almost tossed my proverbial cookies. While they knew I was considering going into the service, I had not mentioned that I had arrived at a decision and that my choice was the Marine Corps. I knew the assumption on their part was that I would gravitate to the Air Force if I decided to enlist. But I felt this was my decision, and mine alone. I didn't want anyone trying to guide me away from it. They had no idea I had spent the day with the Marine Corps recruiter, or that I had signed forms and committed to test for them. The dinner conversation would be interesting indeed.

Chapter 2. The Processing Station

I didn't want to waste the two weeks' time between my visit to the recruiting office and my scheduled processing date in Los Angeles. After breaking the news to my parents, who had both reacted in a strangely quiet manner, I set about preparing for what I perceived to be ahead of me. I decided I needed to prepare not only for the physical challenges that boot camp would undoubtedly have in store for me, but also for the battery of written tests I knew I would face at the processing station. So in addition to the many push-ups, sit-ups, and miles jogged, I also paid a visit to the library and checked out a book that promised to prepare the reader for the armed forces entrance

exams. I spent many hours doing, and redoing the
sample tests in the book. I wanted to ensure that I
not only passed the test, but scored as high as I
possibly could. I wasn't sure how these scores
might or might not impact my enlistment, but I
decided that if I was going to do this, I would give it
my very best effort on all fronts. Who knows what
grades I might have achieved in high school had I
given my studies this much attention? I know for
sure that had I actually studied, I could have taken a
lot of pressure off my chemistry teacher. That poor
man seemed to realize that his grade would make
the difference in whether or not I would be eligible
to dress out with the rest of the varsity team on
Friday nights, and I was always right on the
borderline. Between my pleading eyes, and

whatever pressure the coach may have applied in order to keep his team on the field, I always got the go ahead. But as I now looked back, I regretted that I hadn't come close to realizing my potential and I vowed that I would not short change the Marine Corps in the same way. From this point forward, I would give my best effort in everything I did.

The two weeks passed quickly and I soon found myself saying good bye to my parents, my younger brother and sister, and my girlfriend. It was my assumption that if I passed everything at the processing station in Los Angeles, I would be immediately transported to boot camp at the Marine Corps Recruit Depot in San Diego. I promised my parents and my girlfriend that I would write often, and assured my younger brother that the room we had both shared now belonged solely to him. I think my sister was too young to fully realize that I was leaving and would no longer be a part of the household. She just smiled sweetly and waved as though I was going off to summer camp and would be back in a week or two. I clutched the packet the recruiter had given me and stepped up into the Greyhound bus that was to start me on my way to becoming a Marine.

As the bus hummed along the busy California freeway on its' way to the bustling City of Los Angeles, I opened the packet and reviewed the materials inside. In addition to copies of all of my documents and completed forms, there was a map showing me where the hotel I was to stay in was located in relation to the bus depot in downtown Los Angeles. It was just a few blocks away, but I wanted to be sure I knew exactly where to find it. Getting lost in downtown Los Angeles was not how I wanted to start this adventure. I noted that the processing station I was to report to the following morning was in close proximity to the hotel, so everything appeared to be well planned.

I stepped off the bus in Los Angeles, consulted my map one last time, and entered the busy streets of one of the largest and most populated urban centers in the world. As I walked the few blocks to the designated hotel, I was taken by the contrast of the people on the street of this great city. There seemed to be an equal number of smartly dressed business people hurriedly walking to their next appointment or returning to their offices from the previous one, and people dressed in tattered clothes in need of a bath and a hot meal. Having grown up in a middle class suburban lifestyle, I was not accustomed to seeing people with so many of their basic needs unmet. I felt sorry for those that sat on the sidewalk and offered their hand as I passed by, hoping for a dollar or two. But I had precious few dollars in my own pocket and wasn't sure if I would need them for my own use or not. So I just kept walking, trying not to establish eye contact with anyone I came across. After what were mere minutes, but seemed like hours, I arrived at the designated hotel on my map and my voucher.

As I entered the lobby, I was hopeful that the inside of the hotel was in better repair than the outside. It was not. The walls looked dingy and the carpeting was worn and faded. There was also a peculiar odor in the air. The elderly man at the check in counter had the look of someone whose life had not gone the way he had hoped. There was no smile on his face, or joy in his eyes.

"Checking in?" he asked dryly.

"Yes. I have a voucher," I replied. The voucher contained all the pertinent information.

"Okay, here's your room key. You're on the fifth floor. You can get dinner from five to seven in the dining room with this voucher, and here's another one for breakfast in the morning. The elevator is to your right. Anything else?" he asked.

"No sir. That should take care of it," I replied.

I entered the elevator the desk clerk had

pointed out to me, wondering if maybe I should have taken the stairs instead. The elevator looked, sounded, and smelled like its' best days were far behind it. I decided to chance it and pushed the button for the fifth floor.

After a creaky and slow ride to the desired floor, the elevator finally stopped and the door opened. I stepped out and began walking down a long hallway looking for the room number that matched the key in my hand. As I located my room and inserted the key to open the door, a few young men that appeared to be about my age came out of their rooms and into the hallway. One of them motioned for me to join them.

"You here to process for the military?" he asked.

"Yeah, all of you too?" I responded.

"Yeah, I think the whole floor is guys going into the service," he said. "We're going to take a look around before dinner. Want to come?"

"Sure," I lied.

I had been happy to get off the street and had no desire to return to it anytime soon, but I wanted to fit in with the guys I thought I might end up in boot camp with. So it was back into the elevator and out to the street.

It was suggested by one of the group that we walk to the processing station so we would know where it was in the morning. This sounded like a good idea to me and I was glad I had come along after all. After successfully locating our morning destination, we headed back to the hotel, making note of the fact there was a liquor store nearby and a movie theater just down the street from where we were staying. The film that was playing was the latest John Wayne war movie entitled "The Green Berets" which seemed highly appropriate to us given what we were in Los Angeles to do. Several of us made plans to come back and see the movie after dinner.

I went back to my room and waited for the dinner hour to arrive. The room was small and had a musty smell to it. I wondered when the last time was that they had cleaned the carpet, or anything else for that matter. I was glad I would only be spending one night there. This place was not a vacation destination.

As I entered the dining room when the

dinner hour finally arrived, I looked around and spotted several of the guys I had walked with earlier. I joined them at their table and a hotel employee immediately came over and asked for my voucher. As I presented it to him, I asked about a menu. He replied that there was no menu, we were all to be served the same thing. The "same thing" turned out to be a plate with what appeared to be roast beef, but it had the consistency of cardboard, mashed potatoes that had obviously come from a cheap box of instant potatoes, a serving of canned corn, and a roll that had probably been baked sometime the week before and left out in the open to dry out and harden. Along with that, we were offered our choice of iced tea or coffee. I opted for the coffee, and considered that to be the best part of the meal. At least it was all free, and we were thankful for that. We couldn't help wondering how much the government was being charged for our accommodations and meals. We decided that whatever it was, the government was being ripped off.

After finishing our feast, some of us headed to the theater down the street, while others headed for the liquor store. A couple of the guys were old enough to buy beer and they were planning a little party for their last night as civilians.

John Wayne was my favorite actor by far and I couldn't wait to see his latest movie, especially since the focus was Viet Nam. I knew there was a good chance I would find myself in that country one day and was eager to see what it was all about. But as the movie progressed into some fairly graphic and realistic battle scenes, those of us that had opted for the movie rather than the liquor store were regretting our choice. In one scene in particular, the green berets' encampment was under heavy attack and some of the Viet Cong soldiers became entangled in the barbed wire. Napalm charges were set off and the Viet Cong soldiers were burned to a crisp as we, almost in unison, uttered a quiet "holy shit" and squirmed in our seats. We left the theater wondering what we had gotten ourselves into. Sleep that night was fitful, partly from the lumpy and squeaky bed, and partly from some of the movie scenes. The wake-up call came precisely at 5:00 AM since we had to report to the processing station by the unreasonable hour of

6:00 AM. After the dinner that had been provided, I decided to skip whatever they were serving for breakfast. I was not alone in this choice. As I dropped off my key at the desk, I noticed very few patrons in the dining room.

A group of us walked together to the processing station. The streets were void of the business people at that hour, but the homeless were well represented. Because we were walking in a group, and walking rather briskly, we were not bothered by any of the street dwellers. I was glad I had come with the group, as I suspect a lone walker would have been approached by the men on the street that were down on their luck. There may have been a policeman in the area, but if there was, he was sure keeping out of sight. And some of the street people looked like hard cases.

The processing station was alive with activity. There was no shortage of young men being directed on where to go and what to do. I recall being directed into a large room where I and what seemed like hundreds of other applicants were seated at individual desks to be administered a battery of written exams. It was a long and tedious process, but I felt like I was doing well. All those "college prep" courses I had taken in high school were paying off for me, in spite of the fact I had not given them my full attention. The workbook I had checked out from the library was paying dividends too, as many of the sample questions I had worked on were similar to what I was seeing on these tests. After all sections had been completed and turned in, we were directed to another part of the building where we were to be given our physical examinations.

I had never given much thought to how people come in so many different sizes and shapes, but all of the possible variations were on full display as hundreds of young men moved around from station to station in various states' of undress. We were herded around like cattle at the slaughterhouse, stopping when told, offering our arms for the blood pressure check, reading the eye chart, having our reflexes checked, coughing for the hernia check, and bending over and spreading our cheeks as they looked for who knows what. It was a humiliating process, but at least everyone was equally humiliated. At the conclusion of the physical, we were directed to get dressed and report to the office of the branch of service we were processing for.

Most of the men processing that day were doing so for the Army or the Navy. Very few were directed to the Air Force office and fewer still to the Marine Corps office. I estimated there were maybe twenty Marine recruits waiting to hear some word on whether we passed or not. That was a small percentage of the number that had processed that day. When asked a few times along the way which service I was processing for, I got a head shake and a "you must be nuts," when I said I was there for the Marines.

After an hour or so, a Marine sergeant started calling us one by one to his desk. Some were told that they had not passed either the test or the physical and they were given bus tickets to return to their home towns. Those of us that were told we had passed were presented with even more paperwork to be signed and then told to stand by and we would soon be sworn in. As I waited for the swearing in ceremony, I felt enormous pride in having passed everything and been accepted by the Marine Corps. But in addition to the feeling of pride, there seemed to be a huge knot forming in my stomach as I wondered if I was doing the right thing. Either that, or maybe the "knot" forming was the "cardboard" roast beef from the night before still trying to digest. It was hard to tell. It wasn't long before we were asked to step into a small room to be sworn in. As we stood at our version of the position of attention, a Marine Corps lieutenant in full dress blues walked smartly to the front of the room and told us to raise our right hands and repeat the oath of enlistment after him. Having sworn to defend our nation against all enemies, we were directed back to the Marine Corps office for further processing. I fully expected to be loaded onto a bus and transported to boot camp to begin my training. What I was handed instead was a bus ticket back to Riverside.

"But I thought I passed everything," I said to the sergeant at the desk. "I just took the oath and everything. Why am I being sent home?"

"You did pass everything," he replied. "You were sworn into the inactive reserves just now to hold your place for training. You'll return here in three weeks to be sworn into active duty and we'll

42

ship you to boot camp at that time. We couldn't ship you out today because of the special program you're on."

"What special program?" I asked, not having a clue what he was referring to.

"Check with your recruiter when you get home. He'll tell you about it and give you the bus ticket to come back up here on your shipping date."

I left the office and headed back to the bus depot not only confused, but embarrassed. I had already told everyone I was going to boot camp today and now I would be showing up back at home.

Although my mother was happy that I had received a three week "reprieve", as she put it, I was disappointed. I had prepared myself as best I could

43

and felt I was ready to go. I likened it to going through all the long hard preparation for the big game, and then being told by the coach that you weren't going to play this week. I was never much for sitting on a bench. I was anxious to get into the game.

On the first day of my three week wait, I fired up my Jawa 90 and headed back into town to see the recruiter again. I wondered what special program I was slated for and how that had happened. As I entered the office, the recruiting sergeant stood up and approached me with his hand out.

"Congratulations son," he said as he gave me a firm handshake. "You really scored well on those tests yesterday."

"Thanks," I replied, not letting on that I didn't know I was just down there to test and not to ship out. "They said I was going in on a special program and that you would explain it to me."

"I sure will," he said as he motioned for me to take a seat. "I know we didn't talk about it when you came into the office the first time, but the Marine Corps has an aviation wing in addition to our ground troops. You have to score well to get into the aviation training and a lot of our applicants can't make the grade. So when someone comes along that can score as high as you did, we tell them at the processing station to enlist them under the aviation guarantee."

"But I want to be a Marine," I replied. "If I wanted to be in aviation I would have joined the Air

Force."

"That's the beauty of it," he told me. "You'll still get all of the same training as every other Marine because every Marine is considered to be a rifleman first. But then you'll also get some technical training in the field of aviation and that can help you a lot after you leave the Marine Corps. You get the best of both worlds. And right now, the Marine Corps wants us to enlist as many as we can into the aviation field. There is a shortage there and that's where the Marine Corps needs you the most."

The sergeant made it all sound good, and I felt like I was already committed anyway, so I didn't argue the point even though I had not asked for an aviation guarantee. I was still going to be a Marine and that's what mattered the most to me.

Besides, my parents would probably feel better about me becoming a Marine if they knew I would be working in the field of aviation and not immersed in a deep foxhole somewhere. I left the office feeling good about things, but still anxious to get going. The recruiter gave me a shiny metallic sticker with the Marine Corps emblem on it to place on my motorcycle. I did so proudly.

The three weeks passed quickly and I soon found myself on the bus going back to Los Angeles. And back to the same rundown hotel and cardboard roast beef. Early the next morning, I reported to the processing station along with another group of young men entering the Marine Corps. But this time there was to be no test and no physical for most of us, just a lot of waiting around while our paperwork

47

was being updated and processed. We were told that some of the applicants testing that day would be shipping out with us, so we wouldn't be leaving until they had completed their processing. Those of us that were just there to be sworn in again and shipped out spent the morning trading stories about what we knew about boot camp and how we thought it would be. There was quite a discussion about whether or not the drill instructors could hit us. Several were of the opinion the drill instructors were going to beat the snot out of us during training, while others were equally sure the drill instructors could not lay a hand on us for any reason. I had not given this any thought until this discussion occurred. On the inside, I'm sure all of us were starting to feel the jitters. I know I was. But outwardly, we talked big and showed not one hint of fear.

Finally, we were called into a room where we once again took the oath of enlistment and then we were provided a box lunch and directed to a Greyhound bus that was waiting at the curb in front of the building for us. A rather large packet of paperwork was handed to a recruit seated in the front of the bus and he was told to present it to the drill instructor that would meet our bus at the recruit depot. As the bus merged onto Interstate 5 for the two hour trip to San Diego, we dug into our box lunches and continued with the big talk about how ready we were for boot camp. We were soon to learn, as all of those that had gone before us had learned, that our expectations of what boot camp would be like didn't come even remotely close to

the reality.

Chapter 3. The Arrival

The bus had been quite noisy at times during the trip from Los Angeles to San Diego as the group of young recruits burned off nervous energy by talking big and telling raunchy jokes. But as we felt the bus slowing down and angling toward the off ramp that had a sign clearly indicating "Marine Corps Recruit Depot", the bus got eerily quiet. By the time the bus paused at the entrance to the base, waiting for the military policeman on post to wave us in, it was so quiet that I could hear my own heart beating. The "macho" talk that had been so prevalent during the two hour bus ride had now been replaced with sheer, stark, silent terror. There is no other way to describe it. It was as though the air had been sucked out of the bus and we were all in a state of suspended animation. Nobody moved, nobody talked, and there was scant evidence that anyone was even breathing. As the bus slowly proceeded onto the base and headed to the designated unloading area, we passed by a number of uniformed Marines walking along a sidewalk. Each and every one of them looked up at the bus as we passed by and smiled while slowly shaking their heads from side to side. We couldn't tell if they were taking pity on us, or laughing at us. Either way, it was a clear signal that our lives were about to change in a very dramatic way.

The bus finally came to a stop, set the parking break, and opened the door. Onto the bus stepped the first of several drill instructors that would be responsible for transforming us from civilians into United States Marines. His uniform was impeccable. The pressed creases in his shirt and trousers looked like they would cut you if you happened to brush against them. He had several rows of campaign ribbons over his left pocket with the shiny and distinctive marksmanship awards dangling below the ribbons. But of course the most noticeable feature of his uniform was the stiff "Smokey the Bear" hat with the Marine Corps emblem prominently displayed on the front of it. The hat was tilted slightly forward so that you could barely see the man's eyes peering out from under the rim.

"Welcome to Marine Corps Recruit Depot San Diego," he said in a firm but measured tone.

"Who has my packet?"

A recruit in the front of the bus quickly handed him the packet of paperwork he had been entrusted with. The drill instructor slowly and deliberately removed the stack of papers.

"While at the Marine Corps Recruit Depot, the first and last word out of your mouth will be sir. So when I call out your name, you will respond in a loud and clear voice with "sir, here sir", is that understood?"

"Yes sir!" we all shouted in unison.

"God damn it!" he shouted back at us. "Didn't I just tell you that the first and last word out of your mouth would be sir? Let's try that again. **Do you understand?**"

"Sir, yes sir!" we correctly responded this

time.

He called out each name from the roster on the top of the paperwork he had attached to his clipboard. We dutifully answered in the manner he had instructed us as he called our names until we had all responded. He then peered out from under that intimidating drill instructors hat and began giving us direction, first in the firm voice he had greeted us with, but as he continued, his voice grew louder and louder until he was literally screaming at us at the top of his lungs.

"When I give the word, you will exit this bus and proceed as quickly as you can to the yellow footprints you will see marked on the pavement in front of you. You will find an unoccupied set of footprints and you will stand on them until you receive further instructions. Do you understand?" he said in his firm but measured tone of voice.

"Sir, yes sir!" we answered, hearts beginning to pound.

"When I give the word, you will get your sorry little ass off this bus as fast as you can move! Is that understood?" he told us, his voice clearly rising to a more aggressive level.

"Sir, yes sir!" we shouted back, also raising our voices to a higher level.

The drill instructor then raised his voice to what had to be his loudest and most aggressive tone. He literally looked like he was going to come out of his shoes as he leaned forward and screamed at us. The veins in his neck and face were bulging in unnatural ways.

"WHEN I GIVE THE WORD, I EXPECT EVERY SWINGING DICK TO BE OFF THIS BUS AND STANDING ON FOOTPRINTS WITHIN 30 SECONDS, AND I WILL PERSONALLY KICK THE ASS OF THE LAST SORRY MOTHERFUCKER TO STEP OFF. IS THAT CLEAR?"

SIR, YES SIR!" we screamed back.

"THEN MOVE IT, MOVE IT, MOVE IT!" he screamed as he stepped off and waited at the foot of the bus doorway.

I immediately regretted my choice of a seat near the back of the bus. It was vicious back there as we all threw elbows and pushed and shoved in an effort to make sure we weren't the last one off. I ran out of the bus secure in the knowledge that there were at least two or three still behind me. As I hit the ground running, I followed those ahead of me to the yellow footprints, with uniformed Marines hollering at us every step of the way.

"**MOVE IT, MOVE IT, MOVE IT!**" they all yelled at the top of their lungs.

In spite of the shouting, we could all hear the distinctive sound of a shoe striking the last recruit off the bus squarely in the ass. He went sprawling face first onto the rough asphalt surface, skinning his chin, hands, and elbows. The drill instructor screamed at him to get up and get on the yellow footprints, which he quickly did. He popped up immediately and took his place on a set of footprints, standing there bleeding from his encounter with the asphalt surface of the staging area. It was clear to us at that moment that these drill instructors mean what they say. It was also clear to us that if the drill instructors were not allowed to strike us, nobody bothered telling them.

The drill instructor who had stepped into the bus to greet us now stood in front of the formation that was created by us standing on the yellow footprints.

"Listen up ladies," he directed, back in his firm but measured tone of voice. "Those yellow footprints you are standing on are at a 45 degree angle. This is the proper position of your feet when standing at the position of attention. Once you have your feet in this position, you must then stand straight, shoulders back, chest out, arms at your side with your hands slightly cupped and your thumbs along the seam of your trousers. Your head and eyes will face straight to the front, and you will not lock your knees. Is that understood?"

"Sir, yes sir," we replied.

"Then do it!" he commanded. "Assume the position of attention."

As we all strained to meet the criteria he had just described to us, few were successful in assuming the proper position of attention. The drill instructor, as well as the other uniformed Marines, moved up and down the ranks of the scared recruits and pushed shoulders back, readjusted arms, hands, and thumbs, lifted chins and generally expressed displeasure at the manner in which we were standing. After several minutes of this, a recruit standing in the front rank suddenly fell face first onto the asphalt in front of him. While one of the uniformed Marines attended to the fallen recruit and eventually stood him back on his feet, the drill instructor went back into his maximum volume and attitude mode.

"**DIDN'T I TELL YOU IDIOTS NOT TO LOCK YOUR KNEES?**" he screamed.

"Sir, yes sir!"

"**DO YOU THINK I JUST SAY THINGS TO HEAR MYSELF TALKING?**"

"Sir, no sir!"

"**ARE YOU PEOPLE DEAF, OR JUST FUCKING STUPID?**"

We had no clue how to answer that. Some of us stayed silent, while others answered "sir, yes sir" at the same time the rest were answering "sir, no sir." This infuriated the drill instructor. The veins we had seen just before we ran off the bus were again in evidence and his face was so red it was nearly purple in color.

"**WHAT THE FUCK HAVE THEY SENT ME? YOU IDIOTS CAN'T EVEN FOLLOW A SIMPLE DIRECTION AND STAND AT ATTENTION, AND THEY EXPECT ME TO MAKE MARINES OUT OF YOU?**"

We stood silently while the drill instructor continued to unload on us.

"**I TOLD YOU NOT TO LOCK YOUR KNEES, BECAUSE IF YOU DO, YOU WILL CUT OFF THE FLOW OF BLOOD AND YOU WILL FALL FLAT ON YOUR FACE JUST LIKE THIS STUPID FUCK IN THE FRONT RANK JUST DID! WHEN I TELL YOU**

SOMETHING, YOU HAD BETTER FUCKING PAY ATTENTION AND DO WHAT THE FUCK YOU ARE TOLD. HAVE I MADE MYSELF CLEAR?"

"Sir, yes sir!"

"Being a Marine means following orders," he said, toning it down a notch. "If you fail to follow orders, or otherwise fuck up when you are in a combat situation, you get dead. Not only do you get dead, you get your buddies dead too. My job is to make sure that doesn't happen. From now on, you will do exactly as you are told. Understood?"

"Sir, yes sir!"

"IS THAT UNDERSTOOD?" he yelled at us.

"SIR, YES SIR!" we screamed back.

As he continued telling us what we would be doing over the course of the next several hours, I hung onto every word. It was clear to me that these drill instructors were serious people and this was a serious thing that I had involved myself in. I did not want to make any mistakes or incur the wrath of the man in the "Smokey the Bear" hat in any way. And so it began.

Chapter 4.   The First Night

It was late afternoon when we ran off the bus and assumed our positions on the yellow footprints. We spent a considerable amount of time on those footprints as the drill instructor who had met the bus explained what would be happening next. We were to see our first action at the base barber shop, where we would receive our first Marine recruit haircut, affectionately known as a high and tight. We would then receive an initial issue of clothing, shaving, and hygiene supplies, after which we would be preparing a box in which we would be sending home all the articles of clothing we had brought with us. We would receive an issue of sheets, a blanket, and a pillow case. We would then be marched to our assigned barracks, where we would receive further instructions.

Prior to attempting a move from the yellow footprints, the drill instructor first explained and then demonstrated the essentials of how to march. He demonstrated the pivot required to execute a "right face" or "left face" command. He showed us what a full "30 inch" step looked like. He explained the difference between a "preparatory" command and the command to "execute" a maneuver. He told us that when given the command to "march", we would all step off with the left foot first, taking a full "30 inch" step, followed by the right and then we would pace ourselves according to his verbal cadence. He showed us how we would come to a halt when given that command. He demonstrated everything to us several times.

Once he was satisfied that he had provided us with the information we needed to know in order to move around the base in an orderly fashion, he gave us our first command.

"Right......face!" he bellowed in a loud voice.

As I did my best to execute the pivot and turn to the right as he had instructed us, I was amazed to see that several in the formation apparently had no clue what they were supposed to do. While most of us did in fact turn to the right, some shuffled their feet to accomplish the turn instead of using a pivot motion, some turned to the left instead of the right and then quickly turned around when they realized they were facing the wrong direction, and still others failed to turn at all, apparently too scared to move. This infuriated the drill instructor, who had taken great pains to show us how to execute the maneuver properly.

"Get back! Face the way you were, you fucking morons!" he scowled. **"My God, where do they find people this stupid? Can't you idiots tell your left from your right?"**

"Sir, yes sir!" we responded, apparently too softly.

"I can't hear you.........if you little girls are talking to me, you'd better start sounding off!"

"Sir, yes sir!" we shouted at the top of our lungs.

"Well then, if you can tell your left from your right........there must be some confusion about whether I meant your "civilian" right or your "military" right. This is your "military right" he said as he held up his right arm. "Does everyone now understand which way I want you to turn when I give the command right face?"

"Sir, yes sir!" we dutifully responded.

"Then let's try this again," he stated in a firm voice. **"Right.......face!"**

This time some executed a pivot, some still shuffled their feet, but at least we all turned in the same direction. We did not perform this maneuver in anything that resembled a military manner and we were far from moving in unison as we turned to the right. This did not go unnoticed by the drill instructor, who made some choice and colorful remarks about our lack of military bearing, but he

69

decided we needed to move out if we were to accomplish everything we needed to do before lights out. By turning to the right, we were now in a marching formation consisting of four lines or "ranks".

"Forward......march!" he commanded.

What ensued after his command resembled something you might expect to see in a "Keystone Kops" movie. Some within the ranks stepped off with their left foot as instructed, but we did not do so in unison. Some were waiting for the recruit ahead of them to step off first, and then they tried to step off. Others stepped off with their right foot first, causing then to step on the heel of the recruit ahead of them. The formation contracted, and then spread out, and then contracted again........looking much like a "slinky" walking down a set of stairs. Recruits stumbled and bumped into each other in just the few steps we were allowed to take before the drill instructor came unglued.

Stop, stop, stop!" he shouted at us. **"What the fuck do you people think you are doing? Did you not pay attention when I demonstrated how to march?"**

"Sir, yes sir!" we shouted back.

"Then what was that cluster fuck all about?"

This was not a question we could answer with a yes sir or a no sir, so we correctly stood silent. While this was the first time we heard the term "cluster fuck", we were to hear it many times more during our time in recruit training, particularly in the first phase when we were more apt to make mistakes as a group.

"When I give the command to march, you will all step off with your left foot, your "military" left foot, and you will all step off at the same time. Is that clear?"

"Sir, yes sir!" we replied.

"Then let's try this again ladies........**forward**.......**march!"** he barked out.

The result was only slightly better than our initial effort. We still had the "slinky" effect in play and in no way shape or form did we resemble anything other than a mob of people trying to move at roughly the same time.

"Stop, stop, just fucking stop!" he screamed at us. "We have places to go and things we need to get done, so I don't have time to deal with this right now. We will not march, we will just ditty bop along to where we need to go. Is that clear?"

"Sir, yes sir!"

"Mob........follow me," he commanded in a disgusted tone of voice.

We followed him in what could only be described as a "loose" formation, trying our best to maintain some sense of order. We soon found ourselves in front of the base barber shop, as evidenced by the red and white striped barber pole twirling innocently by the entrance.

"Hippity hop.........mob stop," ordered the drill instructor.

We came to a somewhat organized stop and awaited further direction.

"You will enter the barber shop three at a time, one rank at a time. You will sit in the first available chair to receive your recruit haircut. After receiving your haircut, you will immediately exit the barber shop and assemble on the yellow footprints in front of the exit. Is that understood?"

"Sir, yes sir!"

"First rank, first three recruits.........go!" he ordered.

The first three recruits raced into the barber shop and emerged from the exit in what couldn't have been more than 30 seconds. There was no evidence of any hair whatsoever remaining on their shining white scalps. One had a spot of blood on the side of his head where a growth of some sort had been sheared off during the course of his 30 second haircut. The next three recruits entered the barber shop and emerged just as quickly as the first three had. I had asked for a "butch" haircut before reporting for training, so I thought I was ahead of the game and would just be passed through the barber shop with no further action required. How wrong I was! When my turn came, I ran into the shop and sat in an open chair. The barber draped the barber's cape around my shoulders and went to work on my already shorn scalp. He pressed the clippers against my head so hard that I don't know how an entire layer of skin was not removed in the process. He ran the clippers over my entire scalp in the allotted 30 seconds, and then used a high pressure air hose to blast off any cut hairs remaining. He whipped off the cape and called for the next recruit. I ran out of the shop and found a vacant set of yellow footprints to stand on. I wondered if I was bleeding, as there were several around me that were.

After we had been shorn of our hair, our vanity, and what little remained of our dignity, we formed into a platoon formation by standing on the yellow footprints and the drill instructor then moved us out to our next destination.

We entered a facility designed much like a warehouse. Moving in single file, we passed by a number of uniformed Marines who literally threw various items of clothing at us. The only item in which we were asked about a size was a pair of tennis shoes. For everything else, the Marines issuing the clothing just estimated sizes, always erring on the side of being too large rather than too small. We received a gray sweatshirt with the Marine Corps emblem on the front, socks, tee shirts, utility pants, belt and buckle, a utility cap with the Marine Corps emblem on it, and white boxer shorts. Boxers or briefs was not an option......it was boxers for all.

We then filed into an area with tables where we were told to remove all of our clothing and items we had arrived with, placing everything into a box we were provided with. We then sealed the box and addressed it for mailing to our home address. The only item we were allowed to retain was our wallet. Everything else was sent home.

We left that facility adorned in our first clothing issuance. The pants were too big on most of us and belts wrapped around almost twice. The sweatshirts were big and loose, and the caps were too large for our newly hairless heads. In short, we looked a lot like the clowns that come running out of the tiny car at the circus. Our civilian identities had now been stripped away from us, but we were far from looking like anything even remotely resembling a Marine. It was in this state that we were then "marched" to another facility where we received additional items that we would need such as sheets, a pillow case, towels, soap, and shaving gear. We were given a sea bag (duffle bag) to carry our gear in, and once we had received everything we would need for the first few days of training, we were taken to our assigned barracks to settle in for the night. It was close to 9:00 P.M. when we entered the barracks, but there was still much to learn and much to do before we would be allowed to collapse into our beds for a night of rest.

The barracks was a large building with three levels and six distinct and separate wings. As we were to learn later, we were fortunate to be assigned to one of these barracks affectionately known as "The Hotels" at the recruit depot. Many new arrivals were initially assigned to live in World War II era Quonset huts until space opened up in the newer and more modern barracks we found ourselves in. Since at this point, we didn't even know such a thing as a Quonset hut existed, we were totally ignorant of our good fortune. We were assigned to one of the ground level wings of the building, which meant we wouldn't have to deal with stairs like some of the other platoons did. We were to learn that the recruits assigned to three of the other wings in the building were part of our "series", meaning they were on exactly the same training schedule as we were and that we would be competing with them for various honors as training progressed. The barracks was configured with a large open floor area, with a large room consisting of showers, sinks, and toilets situated at one end. There was also an enclosed office on the same end as the shower room for the use of the drill instructors. The open floor had four rows of metal bunk beds lined up and running the length of the floor. Each bunk bed had two wooden footlockers placed under the bottom bunk.

As long as the day had seemed already, we spent several hours receiving instruction upon arriving at our assigned barracks. We were told we had much to learn, and precious little time in which to learn it. Every day, hour, and minute would be filled with some form of instruction, beginning right now. We were also told to pay attention to every little detail, because the Marine Corps did not tolerate "fuck ups."

We learned that we were officially designated as Platoon 2184. We learned that each platoon consisted of four squads, and each squad was to occupy one row of bunks, with the designated squad leader occupying the bunk nearest the drill instructors office. We learned that we would be trained by three drill instructors and that we would meet the full team upon completion of our processing days.

We were immediately exposed to a lot of new terminology. It was explained to us that we would be using many terms normally associated with the Navy since we were part of the Naval Service and may serve aboard ships at some point in our Marine Corps careers. For instance, the wall was to be referred to as the bulkhead. The floor was called the deck. A mop was called a swab. When responding to an order, we were to respond with "aye aye sir" rather than "yes sir." A drinking fountain was a scuttlebutt. A duffle bag was a sea bag. The shower room was the head. A hat or cap was a cover. The drill instructor's office was the duty hut. A bunk was a rack. The list went on and on. We basically had to learn a whole new form of communication in order to function in our new environment.

We were given very specific instructions and

specifications as to how our racks would be made up. We learned what "hospital corners" were and how to incorporate them into the proper make up of our racks. After many attempts, and resulting angry snarls from the drill instructor as he tore apart racks that were not properly made up, we finally had them put together in an acceptable manner. At least he stopped tearing them apart and moved on to other instructions. We had been issued a pair of flip-flops along with our other gear and we were informed that these were called shower shoes, which also described their primary function. They were required to be worn when showering to help prevent the spread of athlete's foot or other fungal related problems. We were lined up at the end of our racks dressed only in our tee shirts, boxer shorts, and shower shoes. We were told to hold out our hands, fingers spread, and to spread our toes. The drill instructor walked slowly down the lines of recruits checking each one for any tell-tale signs of fungal infections. This was referred to as a hygiene inspection and it would occur every night just before lights out. We sensed that our first day was finally, mercifully drawing to a close. The drill instructor told us that when he gave the order, and only when he gave the order, we would "mount" our racks for lights out. Although there was a clock on the wall near the duty hut, I couldn't see it from my vantage point. I estimated the time to be about 3:00 in the morning. We tiredly waited for the order to mount our racks. Finally, the drill instructor barked out the order.

"Prepare to mount...........ready..........mount!" he shouted.

As we casually started to pull back sheets and blankets to slip into our racks, the drill instructor raised his voice, popped his veins out, and made his eyes bulge in an incredible fashion.

"Get back........get the fuck back to a position of attention!"

We quickly responded, jumping back out of our racks and assuming the position of attention where we had previously aligned ourselves.

The drill instructor paced back and forth as he spoke to us in a now all too familiar stern voice. His eyes focused on one recruit and then the next like a laser beam.

"When I give an order........you will repeat

the order, and then you will say sir, aye aye sir, and then you will execute the order. Is that clear?"

"Sir, yes sir!" we responded.

"I can't hear you!" he shouted.

"Sir, yes sir! We screamed at the top of our lungs.

"And when I give the order to mount, it doesn't mean you take your sweet fucking time and climb into your racks at your leisure waiting for your mommies to come and powder your butts and tuck you in........it means you get into your racks as fast as you can and then you lay at attention and wait for your next command. Have I made myself clear?"

"Sir, yes sir!" we answered in unison.

"I can't hear you!" he shouted again.

"SIR, YES SIR!" we screamed.

"Then let's try that again. Prepare to mount!"

"Sir, prepare to mount. Aye aye sir!" we correctly responded.

"Ready........mount!" he ordered.

"Sir, mount. Aye aye sir!" we shouted as we then jumped into our racks as quickly as we thought was humanly possible. We were wrong.

"Get back........get back.......get the fuck back! Not fast enough ladies. If that is the fastest you can execute an order, you will all die on your first day of combat! You have to be faster. Do you understand?"

"Sir, yes sir!" we screamed as we jumped back into the position of attention.

We repeated the process several times before the drill instructor at long last decided we had complied with his order at a satisfactory pace. We were finally laying on our racks, stiffly, without having been ordered back out of them, awaiting whatever was next. What was next was our prayer instruction.

"Before you ladies go to sleep at night, you will say your prayers. Is that understood?"

"Sir, yes sir"

"You will not say your civilian prayers, because you are no longer civilians. You will say your Marine Corps prayers. Is that understood?"

"Sir, yes sir!" we responded, wondering what a Marine Corps prayer consists of.

"When I give the order to pray, you will pray in the following manner: God bless the President of the United States.......God bless the Commandant of the Marine Corps.....God bless Dan Daly......God bless Smedley Butler.......and God bless Chesty Puller. Is that clear?"

"Sir, yes sir!" we responded, trying to remember the names we had just been told.

"Prepare to pray!" bellowed the drill instructor, who himself must have been tired by now.

"Sir, prepare to pray. Aye aye sir!" we replied in unison.

"Ready........pray!" came the order.

"Sir, pray. Aye aye sir!" we answered and then did our best to recite the Marine Corps prayer out loud. It took several attempts before we were able to recite it to the satisfaction of the drill instructor, but he finally stopped ordering us to repeat it. Surely we would now be allowed to close our eyes and get some much needed rest. By now it had to be close to four in the morning.

"Prepare to sleep," came the long awaited order.

"Sir, prepare to sleep!" we responded loudly and enthusiastically.

"Sleep!"

"Sir, sleep. Aye aye sir!

The lights were turned off and the drill instructor disappeared into the duty hut. At first we just laid there in a state of total and complete silence, most of us probably in a state of shock. Eventually I could hear a few whispers, and then the clear sound of someone trying hard not to cry, but not succeeding in the effort. Our lives had been turned upside down, and to a man I think we were all regretting our decisions to enlist. At that particular moment, we wished we were anywhere but in a rack at the Marine Corps Recruit Depot.

"Who the fuck is Chesty Puller?" whispered the recruit in the rack next to mine.

"I guess we'll find out," I replied. "In the meantime, God bless him."

I closed my eyes and was immediately immersed in a deep, exhausted sleep.

Chapter 5.   Processing days

Before lights out on the first night, the drill instructor had explained to us that the first several days of boot camp would be processing days. Only after we finished processing would we begin our official training schedule. That sounded simple enough when he said it and I thought that meant the first few days would be relatively easy. I thought wrong.

I had fallen asleep quickly when the lights went out, more mentally exhausted than physically, but exhausted just the same. I was in a deep, almost "deathlike" sleep when the world suddenly seemed to explode in bright light and horrific noise. The lights had been turned on and the drill instructor was screaming at the top of his lungs as he threw metal trash cans down the aisles and turned metal racks over, dumping the occupants onto the hard deck.

"GET UP, GET UP, GET THE FUCK OUT OF THE RACK!" shouted the drill instructor over and over again as he tipped over the racks nearest the duty hut. The unlucky recruits that had occupied those racks went sprawling onto the hard, cold deck and scrambled to their feet not really understanding what had just happened to them. The rest of us jumped out of our racks as fast as we could and stood at attention, thankful that we hadn't been assigned a rack near the duty hut.

Once every recruit was up and standing at attention, the drill instructor issued his first order of the day.

"When I give the word, you will make your morning head call, then you will make up your racks as you were instructed to do last night, and then you will dress and assume a position of attention at the foot of your racks and await further orders. Do you understand?"

"Sir, yes sir!" we responded.

"I can't hear you!" came the response from the drill instructor. It was a phrase we would hear often throughout our time at the recruit depot.

"SIR, YES SIR!" we screamed back.

"Turn to on head call!" came the order.

"Sir, turn to on head call!" we replied.

We grabbed the shaving gear and toiletries we had been issued and hurried into the head. After a quick stop at the urinals, some went into the showers while others got in front of a sink and mirror to shave. We had no idea how much time we would have to accomplish our morning head call, but assumed it would be time enough to do what we had to do. We were wrong. After what couldn't have been more than three or four minutes, the drill instructor entered the head shouting at the top of his lungs.

"CLEAR THE HEAD! CLEAR THE HEAD!" he screamed. **"GET THE FUCK OUT! MOVE IT, MOVE IT, MOVE IT!"**

We came running back into the floor area, known as the squad bay as we were to learn, after having accomplished very little of what we had gone into the head to do. Those that had been in the shower were dripping water and trying to dry off as they ran Those that had been shaving were wiping off shaving cream, and in some cases blood from having nicked themselves when the drill instructor interrupted them. We went to work making up our racks as we were instructed, and then dressed quickly in the tennis shoes, sweatshirts, and utility pants we had been issued. All the while, the drill instructor was shouting at us to move it. Finally, we all stood at attention at the foot of our racks.

"You were all issued a sea bag and a combination lock yesterday," said the drill instructor in a measured but firm tone of voice. "Until you are instructed in the proper organization of your foot lockers, you will stow your gear in your sea bag. You will loop the strap of the sea bag around the metal post of your rack and then you will secure it with your lock. Is that clear?"

"Sir, yes sir!" we replied.

"After you have locked your sea bags, you will form up outside, in front of the barracks, in four ranks according to the row you are in right now. This first row is squad number one and will be the first rank in the formation. The second row is squad number two and will be the second rank in the formation. Third row is squad three, rank three. And the fourth row is squad four, rank four. Every time you are told to fall in, you will line up in those same four ranks. Is that understood?"

"Sir, yes sir!" we dutifully responded.

"Then lock your gear and fall in on the road for chow!" came the command.

We scrambled to get our gear into the sea

bags and locked as we were instructed and then ran through the doorway to begin forming up into the four ranks in front of the barracks. It wasn't until we emerged from the barracks that I realized the sun had not yet risen. I had no idea what time it was, but it was definitely pre-dawn, meaning we had probably slept for no more than an hour or so.

In the light emitting from the barracks, the drill instructor spent some time showing us how to space and align ourselves properly when forming the ranks. He showed us once again how to perform a right face or left face maneuver, and reminded us that our first step would be with the left foot.......our "military" left foot.

He then called out a recruit by name and instructed him to step out of the ranks. He asked him if it was true that he had attended college and had participated in the ROTC program. When the recruit responded that he had, the drill instructor designated him as the platoon guide and informed us that in the future we would assemble our formation based on where the guide took up a position. He was presented with the "guide on" which was a wooden pole that flew our platoon banner from it. He then showed the guide where he would stand in the formation, and where he would move to when the platoon was ready to march. Four recruits were then designated as squad leaders and took their positions at the head of the four ranks. The squad leaders seemed to have been selected because of their relative size to the rest of the recruits in their rank. The sun began lighting the area as we prepared to attempt marching once again. Destination, chow hall.

"Right........face!" came the order.

While I would not say our effort was performed well, it was in fact much better than we had done the previous day. Everyone was facing the proper direction, even though the pivot maneuver still proved to be difficult for a number of the recruits. The drill instructor allowed the guide to take up his marching position at the head of the column prior to giving the order to march. We were now properly positioned, properly spaced, and ready to march. We were also quite hungry and more than ready for whatever nourishment awaited us.

"Forward.........march!" came the order.

Although our timing was far from perfect synchronization, at least we all stepped off with our left foot first. We were underway, and in a somewhat organized fashion. For the first time, the drill instructor offered up a simple cadence call.

"Left.......right......left," he called out, repeating it frequently. "Left.....right.....left."

As he called out the cadence, we were better able to synchronize our movements. For just a moment, I remember thinking that we now looked like Marines should look. That thought quickly left me as out of the corner of my eye I saw a platoon of recruits also marching in the direction of the chow hall. They were obviously much further along in training than we were. They wore boots instead of tennis shoes, and wore pressed and starched utilities rather than the baggy sweatshirts and wrinkled utility pants we were adorned with. They were in perfect

101

synchronization, with their sixty or more boots all striking the pavement at exactly the same time. They looked like a well-oiled machine as they moved effortlessly in unison to the cadence of their drill instructor. I remember thinking that our platoon would never look like that.....never. We had guys that couldn't even master the simple pivot maneuver to do a right face, after having been instructed in it several times now. No, in my mind we would never look like that other platoon.

When it became necessary for us to make a right turn, we had not yet been instructed in how to accomplish that. The drill instructor just called out for us to turn to the right, and we bent around in a snake-like fashion. Out of the corner of my eye, I observed that other platoon execute a "column right" maneuver. It looked nothing like what we had just accomplished. "We must look like complete idiots to them," I remember thinking to myself.

As we arrived at the chow hall, the drill instructor brought us to a halt. He formed us into one long single file column in front of the chow hall entrance, where we were to wait for our turn to enter.

"You will stand at the position of attention until you are directed to enter the chow hall!" shouted the drill instructor. **"That means you will look only at the back of the head of the recruit in front of you. You will not eye fuck the area around you.......is that understood?"**

"Sir, yes sir!" we responded.

The drill instructor then strode quickly through the entrance of the chow hall and disappeared from sight.

With the drill instructor safely out of sight, the urge to look around and take in our surroundings was strong. One by one, we all starting turning our heads and checking things out. To our surprise, and horror, we soon realized the drill instructor had walked straight through the chow hall and out a side door. He stood watching us as we gawked around the area in direct contrast to the instructions he had given us. He walked toward us at a very brisk pace as we quickly faced back to the neck of the recruit in front of us. I was about halfway back in the line, and I could see the drill instructor working his way down the line, stopping beside each recruit and saying something to them as he gave each one a little "rap" in the side of the face with his knuckles. Waiting for him to get to me was much like waiting to see the assistant principal in school when you knew you were in trouble. Waiting for the punishment was far worse than the actual punishment you were to receive. Finally he arrived at my side. I stared straight ahead and waited for my fate.

"I told you not to eye fuck the area, but you did it anyway," he said in a soft, almost whispering tone. "Don't ever disobey an order again!"

And then I felt the knuckles rap against the side of my face before he moved on to the next recruit. The rapping of the knuckles really didn't hurt at all, it was just humiliating. I resolved that I wouldn't make that kind of mistake again. If the drill instructor wanted me looking at the back of someone's head, I would stare at that head until the cows came home, or until he instructed me to stop.

Finally, it was our turn to enter the chow hall. It was set up cafeteria style, with the line of recruits moving single file with trays along a serving line, receiving portions of food on their trays from Marines wearing white aprons and plastic gloves behind the counter.

I was hungry, and the food being "plopped" onto my tray looked good to me. As we came to the end of the line, we caught site of our drill instructor seating recruits in rows of tables. As we filed into the row we were directed to, the drill instructor would bark out the order to "sit" and we sat in unison. He then directed us to "eat" and then moved on to seat the next group of recruits. It was an extremely organized process.

I thought we might have a moment of peace to enjoy our meal........I was wrong once again. After just a few bites, I heard the drill instructor already telling the first row that had been seated to "get up and get out".........meaning there would be just a matter of seconds before my row would receive the same instructions. I shoveled as many scrambled eggs down my throat as I could in that few seconds. Then the order came for us to get up and get out. We did so, with most of our breakfast going into a large waste can near the exit door. We ran out of the door and looked for our guide to form up on.

We stood there in our ranks, sleep deprived and still hungry, having just felt the knuckles of the drill instructor on our faces, and waited for the next order. Having learned our lesson, nobody looked anywhere but straight ahead.

The drill instructor emerged from the chow hall and marched us back to our assigned barracks. Waiting there for us were two other drill instructors who had been assigned to our platoon. After a brief introduction, they informed us that they had conducted an inspection of our squad bay and found it completely unsatisfactory. We were told to get in there and get it squared away........followed by shouts to move it!

As we ran into the barracks, we saw that every single rack had been torn apart, with blankets, sheets, and pillows strewn everywhere. Anyone who had not properly locked their sea bag to their rack found it emptied out on the deck as well. As we hurried to remake our racks, the three drill instructors circled around the squad bay shouting and picking out specific recruits to "hover over" as we did our best to try and satisfy them. Try as we might, none of us seemed to be able to make our rack to their satisfaction. A recruit would no sooner finish and stand at attention at the foot of their rack, than one of the drill instructors would pull it apart and bark at the recruit to try again. This went on for quite some time before the drill instructors finally accepted the manner in which we had made up our racks.

As the drill instructor that would be on duty with us that day ordered us to fall out in front of the barracks, the other two drill instructors left the area. We learned that they would be rotating duty days, with one of them being on duty at all times. The duty drill instructor would also be joined by a second instructor on specific training days. Two of our instructors were staff sergeants, and the third one was a gunnery sergeant. The gunnery sergeant was our "platoon commander" and had the ultimate responsibility for training us. We wouldn't see the platoon commander again until after we finished our processing days and began training. It was the staff sergeants that took turns leading us through the processing phase.

Our next few days were filled with things like taking a whole new battery of written tests, another medical exam, being issued more clothing and gear, and getting shots. In between these activities, as time permitted, we continued to receive some basic instruction in drill movements so that we wouldn't look like total buffoons as we moved around the base. We learned to eat as much as we could, as quickly as we could, during our brief visits to the chow hall. We learned to take care of most of our hygiene needs after lights out since we weren't afforded sufficient time in the mornings to take care of everything. After lights out, recruits rotated on a duty called fire watch. We had to have one recruit alert while the rest slept as a safety precaution. Fire watch was done in one hour shifts. We learned to ask one of the fire watches to wake us during the night so we could use the shower, or shave, or even just to have a bowel movement at a leisurely pace. It dawned on me about three days into the process that I had yet to have a bowel movement. I really hadn't had the urge, or the time to take care of this little chore. I had always thought the phrase "scared shitless" was funny and was just used in a joking fashion. I now knew, through personal experience, that a person could quite literally be scared shitless. I was not alone in experiencing this phenomenon, as when I finally got up in the wee hours of the night to take care of this matter, there were several others in the head attempting the same thing for the first time since they had arrived. It took several minutes of intense effort to finally squeeze out several little rock-like balls of shit. It would take several days more before my bowel movements returned to anything even remotely resembling a normal consistency.

The written tests we took were similar to the ones we had taken at the processing station prior to enlistment, but seemed to be more extensive. I assumed this was to verify our earlier scores, and did my best to concentrate on the questions and answer them correctly. We learned that these tests were used to assign each recruit a GCT (general competency test) score, which was then used to assist the Marine Corps in assigning recruits to appropriate occupational fields at the end of recruit training. Once the tests had been scored and GCT's assigned, a few of us were sent to be interviewed regarding an option that opened up to us due to our scores. I was told that my GCT score qualified me to be considered for Officer Candidate School (OCS) upon completion of recruit training. But to be assigned to OCS, I would need to commit to an additional two years on my four year enlistment. I would also need to waive the aviation program I had enlisted under. I had only a few moments to make a decision in this regard. I was not that concerned about waiving the aviation program (I hadn't asked for that in the first place), but I wasn't prepared to extend my enlistment an additional two years before having a chance to experience being a Marine first. I declined this offer, as did the other recruits that had been interviewed with the exception of our platoon guide. He had the ROTC experience in college and definitely aspired to become an officer. At this point, the rest of us weren't even sure we still wanted to be Marines, let alone commit to becoming an officer.

The multiple trips we made to receive shots were not something we looked forward to. They never seemed to tire of injecting various serums into our arms as we walked down a line of Navy Corpsmen armed with "guns" to administer the shots. While most of the shots didn't hurt much at the time of the injection, our arms would tend to get sore as the day wore on. One shot in particular, I will never forget. Instead of the "gun" in the arm, we all received a shot of penicillin by needle in the buttocks. The shot was oil based, and it took days to disperse from the point of injection. It hurt like hell going in, and then it felt like you were carrying a brick around in your ass for the next two or three days. I was grateful that we received only one of those shots.

We were issued many more items of clothing and gear during our processing days, and we received explicit instruction on how to organize our foot lockers to stow everything. We had multiple sets of boxer shorts, tee shirts, green socks, white socks, utility trousers, utility shirts, PT (physical training) gear, and our most prized possession, a pair of black leather combat boots. We were very anxious to get out of our baggy sweatshirts and tennis shoes and start looking more like Marines.

In the evenings, we were instructed in the shining of our brass belt buckles and how to break in and start working on a good "spit shine" for our boots and dress shoes. These would be nightly activities throughout our time in training. We were told to ensure we locked our foot lockers every morning before falling out for chow. Those that failed to do so, would come back from chow and find the contents of their foot locker dumped on the deck. Those that didn't make their rack "tight" enough would come back to find their blanket and sheets on the deck as well. I was pleased that after the first couple of days, my rack seemed to be up to standard and was always still intact when we got back from chow.

We had "mail call" each evening and we were instructed right away to write home and tell our "mommies" that we had arrived safely and were being well cared for. Mail call was something we looked forward to each night, as receiving a letter from home afforded the receiver a brief moment to remember life as it used to be back in the real world. One unlucky recruit received a package from home one evening, and the drill instructor had him open it up in front of the platoon. It contained homemade cookies, and what should have been a welcome sight soon became a nightmare for the recruit. The drill instructor was quite upset that someone's mother would think the Marine Corps was not feeding their son sufficiently. After thoroughly humiliating the recruit verbally, the drill instructor started stuffing the cookies into the recruit's mouth one right after the other, cramming them in when it appeared there was room for not one crumb more. The recruit gagged and had tears running down his face as he tried to chew fast enough to keep up with the onslaught of cookies. When the spectacle was finally over, the rest of us sat right down and wrote a frantic letter home asking...... no...... begging family not to send anything other than a letter. Unfortunately for me, my letter did not arrive home in time to stop my mother from sending me a box of my favorite

chocolate chip cookies. When we saw a package

come in with the letters for mail call, we all cringed

and hoped it did not have our name on it. When the

drill instructor held up the package and called my

name, I felt like I had just been kicked in the gut.

The cookie cramming ritual was not fun, and in fact,

I couldn't eat another chocolate chip cookie for years

after that experience.

During the course of moving around the base

for our numerous processing events, we made note

of several things. We got a look at the obstacle

course, we were shown the wash racks (where we

would be hand washing our clothes), and we were

shown an area near the wash racks that had the

appearance of a rather large sand box. We were told

this was the "pit" and that we would become familiar with it when training started.

And throughout it all, we dutifully prayed each night, God blessing the President, the Commandant of the Marine Corps, Dan Daly, Smedley Butler, and Chesty Puller. It became a running joke after lights out that someone would always whisper "Who the fuck is Chesty Puller?" and we would all chuckle quietly under our breaths. Who indeed. It didn't even sound like a real name.

Without really knowing what was ahead of us in training, we were anxious to get started. These processing days were long and stressful, without giving us the feeling that we were making any progress. We felt much like hamsters running as fast as we could in a wheel going nowhere. And with mean men shouting at us with every step we took. We knew that once we started the training cycle, we would have a specific number of days to get through and we would be able to chart our progress towards graduation. And we were tired of being marched around in sweat shirts and tennis shoes, as those clearly marked us as guys right off the bus that didn't know shit.

We were excited when the drill instructor on duty one night informed us that the following day would be our first day of training. The first phase would consist of three weeks, followed by a week of mess duty, and then we would have two weeks at the rifle range at Camp Pendleton. We would then return to the recruit depot for the final phase of training which would last an additional three weeks. We were to fall out in the morning in full utilities, including our combat boots.

We had been shouted at, stripped of our civilian identities, stripped of our dignity, treated like dirt bags, poked with more needles than one would expect to see in a lifetime, paraded around looking like goof balls, taught a whole new way of speaking, and found out that we could do nothing right. We were good and ready to put this phase behind us and get into the "real" training.

Chapter 6. First Phase Training

I won't attempt to recount each individual day in the training cycle, as many of the training activities we did on a daily basis. I will instead go into detail about the various activities we performed in each phase of our training and give you some insight into how it felt to be a participant.

First phase included a lot of marching and drill instruction, There was also an abundant amount of physical training (PT). We were issued M-14 rifles that we drilled with and learned about on a daily basis. We received instruction in hand-to-hand combat, the military and Marine Corps rank structure, Marine Corps history, and water survival techniques. There were a number of things we were required to memorize, and be able to recall and recite on demand, such as our service number, our rifle serial number, the characteristics of the M-14 rifle, and our general orders. And we learned, often the hard way, that mistakes would not be tolerated, and that a mistake by one was a mistake by all. In short, it became clear to us that we would all succeed or fail as a team. It was drummed into us that if one person makes a mistake in combat, it would impact everyone. So we operated in that same mode throughout recruit training.

We also experienced a great deal of what I will refer to as "mental toughening" throughout our training cycle. It was heaviest during the first phase, but continued to some extent right up to graduation day. From the Marine Corps perspective, they had precious little time to train us and they wanted to put us all under grueling "mental" stress as well as pushing us to the limit physically to see who could take it and who would break. If someone was not equipped either mentally or physically to be a Marine, they wanted to find out about it in this controlled environment rather than later on a battlefield. I recall one of our drill instructors saying that for whatever reason, there are always about 10% that just don't get with the program. I found that figure to be amazingly accurate, as roughly 10% of the recruits that started training with me did not make it through to graduation day. Some cracked under the mental strain, and others could not measure up to the rigorous physical demands. Most of those that "washed out" did so in the first phase of training.

There were a generous number of "mental toughening" opportunities in the first phase of training, particularly in the first several days. As part of our instruction in the proper way to speak, we were told that we would first have to request to speak and be granted permission before speaking to a drill instructor or anyone else in a position of authority. And we were to refer to ourselves and the person we were addressing in the third person. Failure to observe these rules resulted in harsh correction. Done correctly, the process would sound like this: "Sir, the private requests permission to speak to the drill instructor, sir!" If the drill instructor allowed you to speak, he would generally respond with a simple "Speak!"

If a recruit made the mistake of saying "I"
instead of "the recruit" he was confronted by the drill
instructor up close and personal.

"You are not an eye," the drill instructor
would state loudly. "You are a private. This is an
eye," he would say as he poked his thumb into one
of the recruits' eyes and mashed it around until he
was confident he had inflicted enough pain to ensure
the recruit would not make that mistake again. I
managed to avoid this particular mistake, but
roughly half the platoon got to experience the drill
instructor's thumb in one or both of their eyes. If a
recruit made the mistake of saying "you" instead of
"the drill instructor" he also had a close encounter in
which the drill instructor would inform him that "a
ewe is a female sheep........do I look like a fucking

female sheep?"

There were some "no win" routines that we all found ourselves engaged in at some point. A common one was when a drill instructor would single out a specific recruit and started asking questions for which there were no right answers.

"Why are you eye fucking me private? Do you like me?" the drill instructor would ask. If the recruit answered yes, the routine went one direction, and if he answered no, it went in another direction. Both directions led to a dead end after which the recruit would find himself dropping and doing a specified number of push-ups for being such an idiot.

If the recruit responded, "Sir, yes sir!" then the drill instructor would respond in a loud and animated way. "Ooooooh.......well if you like me, then you must love me! Do you love me private?" he would ask. If the answer was "Sir, yes sir!" the routine would continue with the drill instructor asking "Well if you love me, then you must want to fuck me. Do you want to fuck me private?" By now the hapless recruit would realize he had followed this trail to a bad place and he was doomed to receive punishment. "Sir, no sir!" was the only response left........nobody dared respond in the affirmative to that question. "Well if you don't want to fuck me, then you don't really love me do you?" came the question with no good answer. "Sir, no sir!" was the usual response at this point, to which the drill instructor would state "Then you lied to me private, and you hurt my feelings. Why did you lie to me private?" At this point, often times the recruit was so flustered that he would make the "I" mistake and reply "Sir, I don't know sir!" After receiving the thumb in the eye treatment, the recruit would be told to drop and give the drill instructor either a specific number of push-ups, or do push-ups until the drill instructor got tired.

In taking the other track, a recruit fared no better. If in responding to the "do you like me?" question a recruit responded "Sir, no sir!" the drill instructor would answer with the animated "Oooooooh........so you don't like me? Well then you must hate me. Do you hate me private?" If the answer was "Sir, yes sir!" then the drill instructor came back with "Well then, if you hate me, you must want to kick my ass. Do you want to kick my ass private?" At this point, the recruit was in a bad place, and certainly didn't respond in the affirmative to that question, so would respond "Sir, no sir!" which was followed by the whole "then you lied to me" routine. It still resulted in push-ups and a thumb in the eye if you messed up one of the answers.

Another no win situation was when you were told to report to the duty hut in the evening hours. You were to knock three times on the hatch loudly, and then ask for permission to speak. Then you needed to ask for permission to enter, and then you were to stand at attention in front of the drill instructor and loudly state that you were reporting as ordered. No matter how loudly you knocked, or how loudly you shouted, it was never loud enough until at least the third time through the process.

The routine generally went something like

this: knock, knock, knock........"Sir, the private requests permission to speak to the drill instructor, sir!"

"I can't hear you!" would come the response from inside the duty hut. "Is there a mouse at my door?"

After knocking louder, and then raising the decibels in your request to speak to the drill instructor by several levels, you would get the "I still can't hear you!" response from inside. "There must be a little girl tapping on my door!"

BANG, BANG, BANG on the door. "SIR, THE PRIVATE REQUESTS PERMISSION TO SPEAK TO THE DRILL INSTRUCTOR, SIR!" the recruit would holler at the top of his lungs. Finally the response would come, if you were lucky,

"Speak!"

"SIR, THE PRIVATE REQUESTS PERMISSION TO ENTER THE DUTY HUT, SIR!"

"Enter," the drill instructor would answer.

The recruit would then enter the duty hut and snap to a position of attention in front of the drill instructor.

"SIR, THE PRIVATE IS REPORTING AS ORDERED, SIR!"

By this time, the recruit would have extremely sore knuckles from banging on the door several times, and the vocal chords were strained from all the hollering it required to gain entrance. Whatever the recruit was being called in there for, it generally resulted in some form of punishment before the recruit was allowed to return to whatever he was doing in the squad bay. You were never being called to the duty hut for anything of a positive nature. One of the things recruits dreaded the most in the early days of training was hearing their name called along with an order to report to the duty hut. It always meant that there was going to be a confrontation of some sort, and the recruit was highly unlikely to fare well.

Whether it occurred in the duty hut, the squad bay, or outside in formation, if the drill instructor was giving you individual attention it meant that you had not measured up to his expectations in some way. It was stressful enough when he was upset with the entire platoon and scolding us all from in front of the formation, but when he stepped in front of an individual recruit and screamed at him at the top of his lungs from very close proximity (there was generally no more than two or three inches between his nose and yours), the stress level reached 10 on a scale of 1 to 10, with 10 being the maximum level a human being could reasonably be expected to bear. These drill instructors were all schooled well in the art of intimidation and striking fear into the object of their wrath. When you were on the receiving end of one of these close encounters, you literally felt as if your life might end at any moment. It was every recruits' goal to keep these encounters to a minimum. Most of us only had a few of these individual "sessions," but some were not so lucky. There were a few that were constantly screwing up one thing or another, and they found the drill instructor inches from their face often. Unfortunately for the rest of us, the entire platoon would be punished each time one of these individuals screwed up. In fact, there were times when everyone except the offending recruit would be punished.

The offender would get the "face to face" session, but then would be told to stand at ease while the rest of us paid for his mistake with push-ups or some other chosen exercise. This of course resulted in some rather harsh peer pressure in the squad bay that evening. The offender would be confronted by the guide, his squad leader, and usually a few other recruits from his squad once the drill instructor retired to his duty hut. The offender would be told in very stark terms that he had better get squared away, or he would be dealt with. In most cases, this encounter would result in drastic improvement by the offending recruit the following day. But in the case of two recruits that I recall, they continued to screw things up, resulting in the rest of the platoon having to pay the price. The manner in which they were "dealt with" was referred to as having a blanket party.

A blanket party was when, after lights out, the offending recruit would suddenly have a blanket thrown over him that was held down tightly to keep the recruit from being able to move. Several other recruits would then beat him with socks containing bars of soap. Not having been a recipient of a blanket party, I don't know how physically painful the experience might have been, but it was obviously a scary and humiliating event. Unfortunately, the blanket parties that I was aware of did not have the desired effect. Both recruits continued to screw up on a regular basis until they were finally dropped from the platoon and removed from the training cycle. We were never informed about what happened to them after leaving our platoon, we just knew they were there one day and gone the next. In the case of these two recruits, it was a great relief to the rest of us when they were removed from the platoon.

There were a few other recruits that were dropped from the platoon, not because they were screw ups, but because they couldn't pass the physical fitness tests. Those I felt sorry for, because they were really trying hard to measure up but just didn't have the physical strength to make the grade. Those were dropped from the training cycle to a specialized program to help them lose fat if necessary and to build up their strength. I presume most of them eventually returned to training and completed the process of becoming Marines with another platoon.

Then there were a few that cracked under the pressure of the training methods being employed by the drill instructors. I recall one that requested to speak to the drill instructor just before lights out. We could all hear him crying and sobbing in the duty hut as the drill instructor dealt with him in a loud and harsh manner, questioning his manhood, his intelligence, and his lack of guts. The recruit keep sobbing that he just couldn't take it anymore. The next day, he was gone.

Another recruit that couldn't take it anymore chose a different approach. Private Hitchens snuck out of the barracks one night, and somehow ended up at the sleeping quarters of our assigned series officer, a first lieutenant. As we fell out in formation the following morning for chow, we saw the lieutenant approaching our formation dragging Private Hitchens by the ear lobe. Hitchens looked not only uncomfortable, but scared.......eyes bulging and forehead deeply furrowed. Our assigned drill instructor that morning was our platoon commander, the gunnery sergeant.

"Gunny, Private Hitchens here says you've been picking on him. Is that true?" asked the lieutenant sarcastically.

"Picking on him?" answered the drill instructor. "Platoon........have I been picking on Private Hitchens?" we were asked.

140

"Sir, no sir!" responded the platoon in unison.

"That's what I thought," replied the lieutenant. "Take charge of this recruit and get him squared away gunny........I don't want him knocking on my door in the middle of the night again."

"Aye, aye sir," the drill instructor responded. "Fall in Private Hitchens!"

That day became a living Hell for Private Hitchens, as he could seemingly do nothing right and incurred the wrath of the drill instructor at every turn. It was hard to feel sorry for him, as he had brought this on himself. Was he being picked on before going to the lieutenant for help? No more so than the rest of us. We all had our turn at being "picked on" from time to time. Most of us just took it and went about our business, trying to up our game to the point that the drill instructor would "pick on" someone else the next time. Private Hitchens failed the "mental toughness" test. Not only that, he jumped the chain of command and went over the platoon commander's head. He was called into the duty hut that night and was in there for an extended period of time. The next morning, he was directed to pack all of his gear into his sea bag, and he was gone.

As promised, we became familiar with "the pit" during first phase. It was a sandy area near the wash racks behind the barracks and it was just large enough for the entire platoon to stand in it in a very tight formation. If we messed up in drill, or in any other aspect of our first phase training, we ended up being marched to the pit. Once in the pit, we were ordered to do side straddle hops (jumping jacks), or push-ups, or worse yet, bend and thrusts (affectionately referred to as bends and mother fuckers). The bend and thrust is a four count exercise in which you drop down into a squat position, then thrust your legs to the rear ending up in a push up position, then pulling your legs back into a squat before standing back up. It is not a fun exercise under the best of conditions, but in the pit it was pure torture. In close quarters, when the recruit ahead of you performed the thrust motion, his boots would land extremely close to your face, just as yours were doing to the recruit behind you. The boots would kick sand in your face and the action of all of us doing this in the pit raised such a cloud of dust and

143

sand that you could not see and could not breathe properly. While this was an extremely effective "punishment," it also served to toughen us up and demonstrated to us that we could perform physically even in the toughest of conditions if we had to. Trips to the pit were detested at the time, but in retrospect they served a purpose. In fact many of our "punishment" sessions, I believe, were just an extension of our physical training. While we had an ample amount of time dedicated strictly to physical conditioning, the added exercises we did throughout the day for punishment served to enhance our conditioning program. And truth be told, I believe we were often punished for some offense that was completely fabricated by the drill instructor, as we could not detect where or what or who had done anything wrong.

While we performed many different exercises during our PT sessions, we were tested in only three areas as part of the "Commandant's Readiness Test" that all Marines were required to take once a year, and that we had to pass during recruit training. The three events were pull-ups, sit-ups, and a three mile run. There was a minimum standard in each event that had to be met, and an overall accumulation of points that must be accrued. Scoring the minimum in each event would not accrue enough points to pass. You had to exceed the minimum in at least one event in order to pass. With the pull-ups, you had to do at least three, with eighteen giving you the maximum points. With sit-ups, you had to do at least forty in two minutes, with eighty in two minutes giving you the maximum points. The three mile run had to be accomplished in twenty eight minutes, with eighteen minutes giving you the maximum points. I was able to achieve more than the minimum in all these events upon reporting to recruit training, and strived to be able to max out each event by the end of training. I was eventually able to max out the pull-ups, but never quite made it in the other two events. I could get in seventy or slightly more sit-ups in the two minutes, but never made it to eighty. And my best time in the three mile run was about nineteen minutes. These repetitions and times gave me plenty of points to pass, but I was disappointed that I couldn't max out the test, as a few other recruits were able to do in our final test prior to graduation.

The platoon runs that we would do as part of

the physical fitness cycle of our training were difficult at first, but as we gradually worked into shape they became something that I actually enjoyed. The more we ran, the easier it got. Initially, when we finished the run we would be hunched over, gagging and gasping for air. By the end of the first phase, we could cover the ground in platoon formation and still have "gas in the tank" when we were done. We found that when we were in formation, and all our feet were striking the ground in unison, we could move at a steady pace in machine like fashion seemingly forever. The drill instructor would run alongside singing out various chants that we would repeat back to him, and it was all highly motivating. Our run would take us around the end of the runway of the nearby San Diego

Airport and along a chain link fence that separated our recruit depot from the Navy base that also served as a boot camp for sailors. We often did a chant during that stretch if there were any sailors present on the other side that we just loved.

"G.I. beans and G.I. gravy..........gee I wished I joined the navy!" the drill instructor would call out, and we would repeat it back enthusiastically. You could see the sailors on the other side of the fence smile at that........until we then followed it up with a very loud and distinct "Bull shit, bull shit, bull shit!"

Part of our fitness training involved running the obstacle course. The course tested not only your strength, but also your balance and agility. You had to get over, under, and through various different obstacles in a timely fashion. At first, pulling myself

148

up and over a wall was a challenge, but I quickly

mastered the technique. It's amazing how fast you

can learn and adapt when you have a drill instructor

behind you hollering at the top of his lungs and

kicking recruits in the ass if they fell behind or failed

to clear an obstacle.

My favorite was the rope climb. I had good

upper body strength and was able to climb the

hanging rope hand over hand in short order. Upon

reaching the top of the rope, each recruit was to slap

the beam the rope hung from and shout out his

platoon number. Late in the first phase training

cycle, I was really feeling my oats. I was working

into the best shape of my life and cruised through the

obstacle course with ease. One day when I reached

the top of the rope, I not only shouted out "Platoon

2184," I added enthusiastically "The best damn platoon on the whole damn base!" I looked down at the drill instructor on duty that morning and detected a bit of a smile on his face. Several recruits that followed me on the rope picked up on it and shouted the same thing as they reached the top. The drill instructor seemed quite pleased, and we were able to bypass the "pit" without stopping that morning on the way back to the barracks.

From the first day to the last day of first phase training, we drilled at every opportunity. Our marching and rifle drill movements improved some measure every time we went out. In the early days, we received a lot of loud and harsh critical remarks from the drill instructors as we went through the various movements, and always stopped at the pit to be punished for our many marching sins. We spent hours on the parade ground, going over and over whatever movement we were being taught on that particular day. At times, we would be out there for so long that a recruit would find himself in the position of having to make a head call. To keep such interruptions at a minimum, the poor recruit that had to go was humiliated prior to being allowed to relieve himself.

"Sir, the private requests permission to speak to the drill instructor, sir!" the unlucky recruit would holler out.

"Speak!" would come the response.

"Sir, the private requests permission to make a head call, sir!"

"Ooooooooh........the private does, does he?"

151

"Sir, yes sir!" the desperate recruit would shout.

"Is it an emergency, private?"

"Sir, yes sir!"

"Well then.......you better sound your siren and get your warning lights flashing!"

The recruit would then starting making a siren sound and twirling his hand around over his head to simulate the flashing lights. It was never loud enough at first.

"Louder!" the drill instructor would shout. "Louder.......louder.......louder!"

When the recruit finally achieved the proper volume for his siren, the drill instructor would have him run around the platoon formation several times to make sure we were all aware that there was an emergency.

Finally, the drill instructor would tell the recruit to "Go!"

The recruit would run full speed toward the nearest head, siren and lights going all the way. After relieving himself, he would run back to the formation, siren still going loudly. Upon arrival, there were either push-ups to be done as punishment for his interruption, or sometimes the dreaded bends and motherfuckers.

Punishment of this sort was usually meted out in blocks of twenty repetitions. "Drop and give me twenty!" was the most common order. Sometimes the order would come for another twenty. Sometimes the drill instructor would order a recruit to do them until he, the drill instructor, gets tired.

And they didn't tire quickly. But the most dreaded order for punishment was when the drill instructor ordered a recruit to do them "forever!"

The number of repetitions required to satisfy a "forever" order seemed to vary depending on which recruit was being punished. Forever meant you do them until you either, start shaking and fall on your face, or you quiver and strain and are just unable to lift your body weight off the ground one more time. For weaker recruits, forever didn't really last that long. For those that were working into top shape, forever could last quite a long while. My goal when I found myself doing an exercise "forever" was to outlast the drill instructor. By that I mean that I wanted to continue my repetitions for so long that the drill instructor tired of it and ordered me back in formation before I wore out and fell on my face.

Sometimes I actually won the war of wills, and

sometimes I ended up face first on the ground. Either

way, my punishment, added to the regular time

allotted for PT, was a combination that was building

strength in me day by day, punishment by

punishment. I could feel myself being pushed to the

limit, and then realizing that my limit was increasing

daily. I noticed the same thing about the other

recruits in my platoon. As the weaker ones were

dropped from the training cycle, those that remained

continued to grow strong, and to meld into a unit that

was in sync with each other in everything we did.

Toward the end of first phase, we were able to

perform basic drill movements perfectly and looked

like we knew what we were doing as we marched

around the base from one activity to another. Our confidence was growing, and we found ourselves having to stop at the pit less and less.

In addition to all of the drilling and physical training, there were many classes to attend and much to learn. We all carried small notebooks that contained all of our "knowledge" and we broke them out to study whenever we were waiting in line for something or waiting for our next class to start.

There were classes on first aid where we learned to do things like applying a battle dressing to a wound, splinting a broken bone, applying a tourniquet, and covering a sucking chest wound with the wrapper from a cigarette pack. We were schooled on practicing proper hygiene and cautioned about contracting sexually transmitted diseases. We were shown horrifying pictures of human genitals that had been afflicted by some form of venereal disease.

We had classes on the proper care of our weapon. We learned how to breakdown the M-14 rifle into multiple pieces for cleaning and how to reassemble it. We did it over and over again until we could literally do it blindfolded and in a matter of seconds. We learned that the M-14 was characterized as a light weight, air cooled, gas operated, magazine fed, shoulder weapon. After carrying one around all day, I had questions about the "light weight" part of that characterization.

We had classes on hand to hand combat and the art of bayonet fighting. The instructor that came out on a stage in front of us to demonstrate hand to hand techniques looked like he had been chiseled out

157

of a hunk of granite. He wore combat boots, utility trousers, a tee shirt that looked like it had been painted on him (and might not hold together under the strain of his bulging muscles), and his Smokey the Bear hat. To say that he was an intimidating presence would be the understatement of the year. He made it clear to us that we'd better pay attention and master the techniques he would be showing us, because we would one day soon be fighting for our lives in a Viet Nam rice paddy. He demonstrated how to maximize the effect of a punch by putting a twist in it, the most effective kicking and blocking techniques, and how to use everything from our bayonets, to our canteens, to our helmets as a weapon in a hand to hand encounter. He then demonstrated the proper techniques for a bayonet fight. We did the parry and thrust move over and over until it became second nature. We practiced the horizontal butt stroke again and again. He told us that your bayonet may stick in a bone as you thrust it into an enemy soldier, and if that happened, to fire a shot as you pull back on it to help free your bayonet. I remember thinking that this was a useless piece of advice, because if I still had a round to fire, there wasn't going to be any bayonet fight! We practiced everything he taught us at length, adding our best blood curdling scream to every movement to strike fear into our imagined enemy opponent. One point he drove home to us was that in a hand to hand fight, you had to get vicious. The goal was to kill your enemy, as quickly and efficiently as possible. There was no mention of fighting fair, only fighting to win, and doing whatever it took to prevail.

So that we would be in the right mind set to be able to kill another human being in combat, there was a concerted effort to desensitize us. As we entered any of our classrooms, we would stand until ordered to sit. Once ordered to sit, we would first shout out "Kill!" while we were still standing, and then "V.C." as we sat down. The V.C. stood for the Viet Cong, the enemy we would face should we be deployed to Viet Nam.

We had a class where we learned the rank structure and what all the insignias meant, not just for the Marine Corps, for all the other branches of service as well. The Navy rank structure was the most confusing, but one we had to become familiar with since the Marine Corps conducts many joint operations with the Navy.

And we had classes that taught us about the history and traditions of the Marine Corps. These classes quickly became my favorites because I was fascinated by and in awe of the courage Marines had shown in battles and wars throughout history. We learned about the early role of Marines aboard sailing ships, where the term "leathernecks" was first applied to them. They were called that because they wore a piece of stiff leather around their necks when participating in a "boarding" action to help protect their necks during hand to hand saber fighting. We learned how we got the name "Devil Dogs" in World War I. There was a battle raging in France where the Germans had the French army on the run. The Marines were sent in and as the Frenchmen ran past

161

them calling out for the Marines to run for their lives, the Marines advanced fearlessly and fiercely. The Germans were surprised by the ferocity with which these Marines engaged them and called them "Dogs from Hell" which later evolved into Devil Dogs. We learned about the famous battles from the island hopping campaign of World War II such as Iwo Jima and Tarawa. We were made aware of "The Frozen Chosin" battle in the Korean War, where Marines had to fight their way from the Chosin Reservoir back to their lines through a numerically superior force and the most brutally cold and frozen conditions one could imagine. And we learned about the current role of the Marines in Viet Nam and heard some of the exploits of more recent heroes.

And finally, we learned about the men we

had been praying for every night. The Marine Corps legends of past wars, Dan Daly, Smedley Butler, and of course the man with the name we didn't think was real, Chesty Puller. Once we had learned about the men behind these names, and what they had done to earn their place in Marine Corps legend, we prayed for them with much more reverence than we had done before we knew who they were.

Although Chesty Puller was, and continues to be, the most famous name from Marine Corps history, it was the story of Dan Daly that fascinated me the most. Maybe it was because he was just a private when he won his first of two awards of the Medal of Honor. It seems that Private Daly was assigned to a detachment of Marines guarding a diplomatic post in Peking, China in the year 1900.

During the "Battle of Peking" known as the "Boxer Rebellion" the diplomatic post came under attack from the "Boxer" rebels. There was a breach in one of the outer walls of the compound, and Private Daly was assigned to guard that breach throughout the night. He was told he couldn't allow anyone to enter the compound through this breach, and he would have no support in this assignment as the other members of the detachment were needed to fortify other areas. He was armed with a machine gun, a rifle, a pistol, and a knife. As darkness covered the compound, the boxers decided to probe the area where they saw a breach in the wall to see if they could overwhelm whoever was guarding it and gain entrance to the inner area of the compound. Sounds could be heard through the night of machine gun fire from Daly's position, eventually evolving into rifle fire as he ran out of ammo for the machine gun. Then pistol fire took over as he ran out of bullets for his rifle, and then as dawn approached, there were no sounds of gunfire at all, only an occasional scream. When the detachment leaders went to check on him at daybreak, they found him still guarding the breach, now armed only with his knife. The body count of boxers who had tried to enter the compound through Private Daly's position exceeded two hundred. I was absolutely in awe as the history instructor related this story. It had been two hundred armed rebels against one Marine Corps private, and the private prevailed. If you were to look up the phrase "bad ass" I'm quite sure there would be a picture of Dan Daly next to the definition.

Fifteen years later, as a gunnery sergeant, Daly was awarded another Medal of Honor for heroism in a U.S. action in Haiti. He also received a Navy Cross for his actions in World War I in France in the year 1918. As a first sergeant, he is credited with yelling "Come on, you sons of bitches, do you want to live forever?" during the battle of Belleau Wood as he led a fierce charge against a German position. He eventually rose to the rank of sergeant major, before retiring in the year 1929.

Smedley Butler was another Marine who had been awarded the Medal of Honor twice. He also had three other medals for heroism. His first Medal of Honor was due to heroic actions on his part during the Battle of Veracruz, Mexico in 1914. He won his second for actions in Haiti in 1915 and joined Dan

Daly as being the only two Marines to receive a Medal of Honor twice for separate actions. He eventually rose to the rank of major general before retiring in 1931.

Chesty Puller is the giant of Marine Corps legends. A mixture of facts and legendary stories about Chesty has elevated him to a level occupied only by himself. He is considered the "Marine's Marine" and was known as an officer that sincerely did his best to improve the conditions for his enlisted men. He didn't "send" men into combat, he "led" them into combat. He is the only Marine to have been awarded five Navy Crosses.

As a young lieutenant, Chesty won his first Navy Cross for leading his forces against armed Nicaraguan bandits in 1930. He led his troops in five successful engagements against forces with superior numbers. He won his second Navy Cross while still a lieutenant serving in Nicaragua in 1932, again defeating armed bandits with superior numbers. His third Navy Cross was earned while serving as a lieutenant colonel in the battle for Guadalcanal in World War II. Under Chesty's leadership, his battalion held a crucial position against a Japanese force with superior numbers who had launched a vigorous and vicious attack against the Marines. His fourth Navy Cross was also awarded for action during World War II. As a lieutenant colonel, he served as the executive officer of a battalion of Marines engaged in battle in New Britain. After the commanding officer was wounded, Chesty assumed command and repeatedly exposed himself to enemy fire as he directed his troops in battle and eventually won the engagement. His fifth Navy Cross was won in Korea in 1950. He was then a full colonel and the commanding officer of the First Marines, First Marine Division. In action near Koto-ri, Korea, Chesty moved throughout his troops, providing direction and assisting them however he could, as they withstood repeated and heavy attacks. His actions inspired his men and they successfully kept open a critical supply line. He personally supervised the evacuation of all the casualties. He reached the rank of lieutenant general before retiring in 1955 as the most decorated member of the Marine Corps.

Learning about these heroic Marines was very thought provoking. It made us wonder if we would "measure up" to the high standards they had set for us. When our time came, would we be able to show the same kind of courage these Marines had? We felt the pressure to train hard and be ready for whatever waited for us in our Marine Corps journey. We did not want to disappoint the likes of Chesty Puller.

Our water survival training consisted of a day at the base swimming pool learning techniques for jumping from the side of a ship and surviving for an extended period of time in the water should those things ever become necessary. I was a strong swimmer and had no fear of the water, but I did have an issue with jumping off the thirty foot platform that simulated jumping from a ship into the ocean. As a young "pre-teen" man, I had once decided it was time for me to try going off the high dive at the local city plunge. I confidently climbed the ladder and walked out to the end of the board. But when I looked down through the clear pool water and saw the drain cover at the bottom of the deep end, it looked to me like I would be jumping from a height roughly equivalent to the Empire State Building. I froze. When other kids started hollering at me to jump or get out of the way, I swallowed my pride and got out of the way.......climbing back down the ladder to the sound of laughter from some of the older kids. It was a humiliating experience and I never climbed up to the high dive board again. Until now.

Instructors demonstrated the position we would assume when jumping. We were to step off feet first, legs crossed, with one hand cupping our vulnerable "private parts", and the other hand cupped over our nose, and ensure that we hit the water feet first in an upright position. This did not seem difficult, but as I climbed the ladder to wait for my turn to jump, the high dive experience came to mind and I wondered if I would be able to do it. It turned out that the fear of what the drill instructors might do if I failed to jump outweighed my childhood fear of the high dive. When my turn came, I assumed the proper position and stepped off without hesitation.

We were also shown how to remove our shirts and/or our pants and tie off the arms or pant legs so we could inflate them and use them like a life preserver. We practiced this technique again and again. Then we were shown a technique that would enable us to survive for an extended period of time without tiring us to the point of exhaustion. You basically went limp just below the surface, and then used a little kick and slight arm motion to raise your head out of the water to take a new breath when you needed to, and then relax beneath the surface again to conserve energy. I was able to master this technique rather quickly and could have spent the rest of the day in the pool (it was sure preferable to doing bends and motherfuckers in a sand pit), but there were others that struggled mightily after several minutes in the water.

There were numerous water instructors around the pool, as well as the drill instructors who had marched us to the pool. I'm sure they would have intervened if a recruit was actually in danger of drowning, but for the several recruits that were having great difficulty in the pool you would have trouble convincing them that the instructors had their best interest at heart. The water survival stroke was a timed exercise, and there were a few that were struggling with it that attempted to swim to the side of the pool to either hang on to the edge or to get out of the water prior to time being called. They were met at the edge of the pool by an instructor hollering at them and using their foot to push them back into the water. I'm sure those particular recruits were convinced that the instructors meant to drown them, as some of them tried hard to fight off the instructors and push their way out of the pool. None were successful in leaving the pool early, and none of them actually drowned. So I guess they learned, the

174

hard way, that they could survive in water much longer than they thought they could. There was one recruit, however, that was coughing up water when he was finally allowed to roll up on the edge of the pool. He was a large man, much larger than the instructor who stood over him berating him for his pathetic water skills. When he finished coughing up water, he must have been convinced the instructor had sincerely tried to drown him, as he grabbed the surprised instructor and threw him to the deck beside the edge of the pool. He jumped on him and landed several hard punches to his face before the other instructors swarmed him and pulled him off. He was roughed up pretty good by the instructors coming to the aid of their partner, and then led away. We never saw that recruit again, and never heard what had

175

happened to him. The rumor was, he was buried in the "pit" by the wash racks. Although obviously untrue, it was a great rumor and was repeated often.

I was grateful for my grandmother having taken me to swimming lessons every morning one summer when I was a kid. As a result of all those cold mornings at the plunge, I was at home in the water and that had paid off big time for me during this particular training activity.

One last activity that we became active in near the end of first phase was pugil sticks. This was an activity designed for us to practice our bayonet fighting techniques. The pugil sticks were wooden poles, roughly the length of a rifle, and had large pads on each end. They also had padded openings for your hands to go through and grasp the poles.

Each combatant was equipped with a helmet much like a football helmet, and a padded harness to protect the groin area. The pugil stick bouts were held in a sandy area where the platoon would form a ring in which the combatants would go at each other. The drill instructor would blow a whistle to start the match, and two recruits would charge at each other and engage in physical combat using the pugil sticks as their weapons. The match would end only when the drill instructor blew his whistle a second time, usually not until one recruit was on the ground absorbing numerous blows from the other.

Having played football in high school, I was not afraid of "contact" and really thrived in this particular drill. I was super aggressive when the whistle blew, rushing at and through my opponent if he hesitated in any way. I was quite good at throwing an initial thrust, and then coming across with a strong horizontal butt stroke that generally knocked my opponent to the ground where I would continue striking him with side to side strokes until the whistle blew. Our first couple of sessions with the pugil sticks ended with me getting the better of everyone I was matched against. This did not go unnoticed by the drill instructors, as I heard positive comments from them on several occasions regarding my aggressiveness.

As first phase was nearing the end, I was feeling good about things. I thought I had reported to boot camp in good physical condition, but now felt much stronger than the day I reported for training. We were making a lot of progress as a platoon as well, being marched to the "pit" less and less as time passed by. While we still had improvements to make, we at least looked like an organized body as we marched around the base. And although their mood could turn on a dime if we made a mistake, the drill instructors seemed to be satisfied with our progress most of the time now. In just a couple of days, we would be wrapping up our first phase of training and packing our gear to go to Camp Pendleton for the rifle range. We would also be doing our week of mess duty while at the range before returning to the recruit depot for our final phase of training. My spirits were high, and I was one very motivated recruit.

On our next to last day of first phase training, we marched out to the pugil stick area for one last go at each other. I was all pumped up and looking forward to the bouts, as I felt this was an area where I could really shine. When my first turn came, I put the safety gear on and waited for the whistle to blow. Upon hearing the whistle, I charged at the recruit on the other side of the ring and quickly landed a hard blow to the side of his helmet, knocking him off his feet. I stood over him swinging my pugil stick from side to side landing blow after blow. During the action, my right hand slipped off the stick and came out of the padded protection. They had told us that if this happened, we should stop, turn our back and take a few whacks from our opponent if necessary, but to get our hands back in the pads before continuing to fight. Because I had a distinct advantage in the fight, I was unwilling to let up in

180

order to get my hand back inside the padding. I just grasped the outside of the pugil stick and kept pounding my opponent until the whistle finally blew. I got back in line very pleased with my performance and eager for the next bout, totally unaware of the fact that when my opponent was down, he had kicked up at me and the edge of his boot apparently struck the back of my exposed right hand.

When it was nearly my turn to go again, I tried to get the gear on and found that I couldn't close my right hand. I looked down at it and was horrified to see it swollen up to at least three times its normal size. I wasn't in any pain, so I kept trying to close it into a fist, but with no success. The recruit standing next to me saw it and uttered "oh shit!" under his breath. "You better show that to the drill instructor," he told me. Since I couldn't grasp the pugil stick and it was almost my turn to enter the ring again, I had no other choice. I fell out of line and approached the drill instructor on duty with us that morning.

He didn't look at me as I approached him, keeping his eyes focused on the pugil stick bout currently underway.

"Sir, the private requests permission to speak to the drill instructor, sir!" I barked out in a loud voice.

"Speak," he replied without looking at me, eyes still focused on the bout.

"Sir, the private thinks he broke his hand, sir!" I shouted.

"Ooooooh.........the private does, does he?" he

replied sarcastically, still not looking at me.

"Sir, yes sir!" I responded, holding my hand out for him to see.

He finally turned his head slightly and looked down at my hand. He did a slight "double take" motion with his head and eyes, with his eyes bulging out a bit. There was always an ambulance on site in case of an injury during these pugil stick bouts, and the drill instructor ordered me to report to it right away. As I headed for the Navy Corpsmen manning the ambulance, I heard the drill instructor say the word "shit" in a disgusted tone of voice.

I spent the rest of the day at the nearby Naval Hospital, getting x-rays taken and having a cast put on my right hand. The corpsman taking the x-ray told me to lay my hand flat, which I did as best I could. It wouldn't lay completely flat, as hard as I tried, so the corpsman came over and pushed down hard on the back of my broken hand to flatten it out. This caused me a great deal of pain, but I would be damned if I was going to let any Navy corpsman know how much he hurt me, so I just gritted my teeth and took the pain while he shot the x-rays. The bone connecting to the middle finger on the back of my right hand was clearly broken in the x-ray. I was outfitted with a hard cast that ran about halfway up my forearm. They told me I would need to wear the cast for four weeks, and then they took me back to my barracks to rejoin my platoon at the end of the day. I went to sleep that night having no idea what the future held for me now. How was I going to fire my rifle at the range with a cast on my right hand?

Chapter 7.   Medical Rehabilitation Platoon

The next morning, when the platoon returned from chow, the drill instructor gathered us all in the squad bay to explain what we would be doing that day in preparation for going to Camp Pendleton the following day. As he was explaining everything, he suddenly looked right at me.

"You know you're not going with us don't you Andrews?" he said very coldly.

"Sir, yes sir!" I lied. I had no idea whether I was going to go with them or not. Apparently, it was not. When the rest of the platoon went out for PT and drill, I was directed to pack my sea bag and report to the Medical Rehabilitation Platoon, known as MRP. I was being dropped from my platoon and the training cycle, and I felt like I had just absorbed a hard kick to the gut. In the flash of a single moment, I had gone from being a highly motivated and squared away recruit, to a "broken" recruit being dropped and sent packing. I was devastated.

I was to spend a month in MRP before I would get my cast removed and tested for a return to training. Life in the MRP was quite different from a training platoon. There were maybe thirty or thirty five recruits in MRP at any given time while I was there. About half of the recruits were there as a result of a training injury and were anxious to heal and get back to the business of becoming a Marine, like myself. The other half were recruits that were trying to use their injuries, real or imagined, to get a discharge and get the hell out of there. They were a sad lot to be around, and I often wondered why they had signed up in the first place.

One of my first tasks after getting settled in and assigned to a rack was to write a letter home with my new address. Since I was right handed, and it was my right hand that was now encased in plaster, this was no easy task. I had never attempted to write left handed before, and my first few tries were completely unreadable. I finally managed to scrawl some words that could be read, although they looked like the work of a pre-school tot. I assured my parents that even though I had a broken hand, I would be fine and would return to training in a month. I asked them to give my new address to my girlfriend and explain to her what had happened. I sent off the letter, and by some small miracle, it made it to my home address.

My mother told me later that she had quite a time trying to make sense of the scrawls on the paper she received from me. By the time my cast came off, I had become fairly efficient at writing left handed.

While there, recruits were assigned to various tasks depending on the nature of their injury. Since I was fully mobile, I was often assigned as a "runner" during daylight hours. I would stand at rest in a headquarters building until summoned by one of the Marines there to "run" a package or folder of papers to another part of the building, or to another building elsewhere on the base. I actually enjoyed being deployed on a task where I had to deliver something to a building on the other side of the base. It gave me a chance to get familiar with where everything was, and I could move around without a drill instructor watching my every move. I had a certain amount of "freedom" that I had not experienced since first climbing off the bus and finding a set of yellow footprints to stand on.

I was less enthusiastic about some of the other assignments. I'm not sure what those with leg or foot injuries found to do while they were rehabilitating, but those of us that could stand did a lot of "fire watch" duties in addition to being runners. Sometimes it was fire watch for our own MRP, but at times we were sent to stand fire watch for the Correctional Custody Platoon as well. Those were recruits that had committed some sort of offense that warranted more than a trip to the pit or doing bends and motherfuckers forever. Most of them, I believe, were to be discharged from the Marine Corps for various

189

reasons. But while they waited for a final disposition, the Marine Corps put them through pure hell in that Correctional Custody Platoon. Their drill instructors, and their daily routine, made the training I had been through look like a walk in the park. I'm not clear on what activities they participated in during the course of the day, but it was obviously hard labor, as those young men were totally exhausted when they turned in at night. And they were rousted out of their racks well before daylight every morning in a very loud and rude manner. They had drill instructors shouting in their ears from the moment they got up until the moment they were finally allowed to close their eyes. I could feel the tension in the room even as they slept when I walked fire watch for them. I don't know what those poor souls had done, but they were sure paying

190

a heavy price for it.

Fire watch for MRP was less stressful on most occasions, but one night proved to be quite interesting. As I stood my watch in the middle of the night, I heard a recruit call out softly for the fire watch. As I approached him to see what he wanted, he turned on a light to show me what he had done to himself. This recruit was one of those that wanted out in any way he could make that happen. Apparently, whatever injury he had wasn't going to get it done, so he decided to take action. He had slit his wrist with a razor blade and held it out for me to see. There was a substantial amount of blood dripping from his wrist.

"Look what I did," he said calmly. "Go get the drill instructor."

I was not thrilled with the idea of waking up a

drill instructor in the middle of the night with news such as this, but I didn't see what other option I had. So I went to the duty hut and banged hard on the hatch three times.

"Sir, the private requests permission to speak to the drill instructor, sir!" I shouted at the closed door as loudly as I could.

"What in the fuck do you want?" came the gruff response.

"Sir, the drill instructor is needed on deck, sir!" I called out.

"This better be fucking good private!" he growled at me as he opened the door and stepped out wearing only his shower shoes, his boxer shorts, a tee shirt, his Smokey the Bear hat , and a scowl on his face.

"Sir, one of the privates cut his wrist sir!" I reported.

"Oooooooh........ he did, did he? Show me where this stupid mother fucker is!"

I led him to the rack where the private with the bleeding wrist calmly awaited the arrival of the drill instructor. He held it out so the drill instructor could get a good view of it.

"Die mother fucker........die!" he said with enthusiasm, and then turned and strode back to the duty hut leaving the shocked private sitting on his rack stammering "But sir......but sir."

I couldn't believe what I had just witnessed myself. It was the coldest thing I had ever seen. Of course, the drill instructor called for an ambulance as soon as he returned to the duty hut, and the recruit with the slit wrist was dealt with promptly. But not before getting quite a scare from the drill instructor. It was obvious the recruit had no desire to actually die, he just wanted to get out of the Marine Corps. The following morning, the drill instructor held class for the rest of us, showing us how to slit your wrist properly if you really want to end it all. He didn't want us wasting his time if we weren't serious about it. We never saw the recruit with the slit wrist again, so I assume his effort to get out of the Marine Corps at any cost was successful.

There was one recruit in the unit that was a little larger than most of us, and he liked to throw his weight around as if he was in charge whenever the drill instructor wasn't close by. He had some sort of foot problem that landed him in MRP, so he spent most of his time in the barracks during the day with the other recruits that had mobility issues. Those of us with hand, arm, or shoulder injuries were not subject to his antics since we were assigned to outside duties during daylight hours, and the drill instructor was always in close proximity in the evening hours leading up to lights out. But one night, the drill instructor seemed to be preoccupied with something in the duty hut and he wasn't paying much attention to what we were doing out in the barracks. The bully decided to expand his reach to those of us with upper body injuries. The first recruit he decided to pick on had a cast on his right forearm similar to mine. I guess the bully reasoned that since he had two good arms, and the subject of his attention could only use one, he could have his way with him with little

195

resistance. It was a big mistake on his part. After being told by the recruit with the cast to "get the fuck away from me," the bully struck a fighting pose and prepared to deliver a blow. His intended victim threw his left hand straight out to his side, which distracted the bully for the brief moment it took for the recruit to swing the arm with the cast on it across like a horizontal butt stroke with a rifle. The cast must have felt like a baseball bat striking him in the head, as the bully hit the deck hard. He got up dazed, surprised, and in no mood to try his luck again. When told again to "get the fuck away from me," he complied without a word. He never challenged anyone with a cast again.

The thirty days passed as if each day was in slow motion and the end of it would never arrive.

Since we had more free time in the evenings than a training platoon, I did get to know and became good friends with two of the other recruits. One was from Ohio and had enlisted as a reserve, and the other was from New Orleans. I thought my friend from New Orleans had the coolest accent I had ever heard and could listen to him talk all day long. As my thirty days finally passed, and I was sent to the hospital to have my cast removed, I knew my friends were close to returning to duty as well. But I would be the first to leave, and as anxious as I was to get back to training, I knew I would miss my new friends.

The day after my cast was removed, I was given a physical fitness test to ensure I was ready to stand up to the rigors of training. I knew I could do enough sit-up repetitions, and was still in good

197

enough shape to complete the run in a timely fashion. I was concerned about doing the pull-ups however, because my grip was weak after my hand was completely immobilized in the cast for a month. When I jumped up onto the pull-up bar, my grip with the right hand was weak but my determination to get back to training was strong. I managed to keep my right hand on the bar and basically did one armed pull-ups with my left arm. The right hand was just for show. I couldn't do many pull-ups like that, but I did enough. I passed my test and was designated fit for duty. That afternoon I said good bye and good luck to my two friends, hoping to cross paths with them again. I packed my gear into my sea bag and reported to my new platoon for resumption of training. I had been dropped from Platoon 2184, and was now assigned to Platoon 2204 exactly a month later. My new platoon was at nearly the same point in training as my first platoon had been when I left it. I knew there were many adjustments for me to make. How would my new drill instructors be in comparison to the ones I had before? What kind of reception would they give to someone who had been dropped from their original platoon? How would the other recruits in my new platoon receive me? Would I regain the strength in my right hand or would it hamper me through the rest of boot camp? These were all things that raced through my mind as I made my way to the barracks of my new platoon.

Chapter 8.   Back to Training

When I arrived at the barracks I had been directed to, a drill instructor awaited me in the duty hut. I knocked on the hatch and stated that I was reporting as ordered. He took my packet of paperwork and looked it over very carefully. He then showed me where my rack was and told me to stow my gear. The platoon was in the field and would return shortly to get ready for chow. He would introduce me to the guide and my squad leader at that time.

As I finished stowing my gear in the assigned footlocker and making up my rack, the platoon came to a halt in front of the barracks. They fell out of formation and came running into the barracks to lock up their rifles and clean up in preparation for going to evening chow. The guide, my new squad leader, and I were called to the duty hut for brief introductions. Upon leaving the duty hut, the squad leader walked with me back to the squad area and introduced me to the rest of the squad I had been assigned to. There was little acknowledgment of my existence from any of the squad members, as they were busy doing what they had to do prior to going to chow. The squad leader, however, did take me aside and told me how it was going to be.

"You better not be a fuck up," he said. "We just dropped a couple of fuck ups from my squad and I don't need any new ones. I'm getting tired of being called to the duty hut every night to pay for other peoples fuck ups. Do we understand each other?"

"Don't worry about it," I responded. "I'm not

201

a fuck up."

"Why did you get dropped from your first platoon?" he asked.

"Because I broke my hand in pugil sticks," I replied. "I've been in MRP with a cast on my hand for the past month, but I'm good to go now. I can carry my own weight, so don't worry about being called to the duty hut on my account."

"We'll see," he said with a bit of attitude, and then went about his business.

After evening chow and mail call, we had some free time to work on shining our brass, spit shining our shoes, and writing letters. During this time some of the other members of my new squad made conversation with me. They were interested in what had happened to me and where I had been before joining their platoon. They seemed less suspicious of me than the squad leader and made me feel somewhat welcome.

As we engaged in the training schedule the following day, it became apparent to me that I would be repeating a few training days that I had already completed with my prior platoon. That meant returning to the scene of my misfortune, the pugil stick arena. I had mixed feelings about it since it was something that I had excelled at, but had suffered a set-back as a result of. It was something I had to do, so I resolved not to worry about it. As we marched between the various training activities and classes, and while in class, I constantly opened and closed my right hand to try and regain strength in my grip. I could feel it getting stronger by the hour and after just a couple of days had full confidence in it again. Just in time for my return to the pugil stick contests.

I had been able to keep up in the physical training with no problem, and performed drill movements without a hitch, drawing little to no attention from my new set of drill instructors. Even the squad leader had come to the conclusion that I would not be a problem for him, as he paid very little attention to me.

Finally, we were marched to the pugil stick area and formed into that familiar circle. I felt that little knot that forms in your stomach as the nerves kick in, much like when you are on the football field waiting for the kick off. Just as the knot would go away once the ball was in the air in football, I felt the knot disappear once I donned the protective gear and heard the whistle blow to start my first match.

I charged aggressively toward my opponent, letting out my best blood curdling scream. I successfully landed my first thrust and followed it with a horizontal butt stroke that dropped him to the deck like a sack of potatoes. I attacked the fallen recruit and kept landing side to side strokes until I heard the whistle blow.

The drill instructor gave me a nod of approval and bellowed out "Out fucking standing!" as I returned to the line to wait for my next match. I had been apprehensive about returning to this activity, but now I was glad to have this opportunity to prove myself to my new drill instructors and fellow recruits.

I won every match I engaged in during this session and was highly motivated as we left the pugil stick area to move on to other training activities. I had caught the eye of the drill instructor in a positive way, and had proven to my fellow recruits that I was not a fuck up. I had also proven to myself that my grip would not be a problem going forward. I was ready to once again fully immerse myself in the training and work towards graduation day with enthusiasm.

On our next to last day before completing first phase, we once again found ourselves at the pugil stick area engaging in hand to hand combat. It was our platoon commander, a gunnery sergeant that took us out for this final exercise. I welcomed the chance to show him what I could do and couldn't wait for my first opportunity.

I was just as successful during this session as I was in the first one. I came out aggressively and loudly every time the whistle blew and managed to ground my opponent in every match. This did not go unnoticed by the platoon commander, who also thought my performance was "Out fucking standing!" As we left the pugil stick area for the final time, I felt good about what I had accomplished in that particular training activity and looked forward to whatever was next.

What was next came as a complete surprise to me. That evening I was called to the duty hut, along with my squad leader and the guide. As we stood at attention, the platoon commander zeroed in on my squad leader with a laser like stare.

"Private Masters," he scowled. "You have not met my expectations as a squad leader. You are not aggressive enough and your squad doesn't respect

207

you. You're fired!"

He then focused on me.

"Private Andrews," he said in a raised voice.
"You showed me something today. You have the kind
of fire in your belly I want to see in my squad leaders.
You're hired!"

"That's all," he barked. "Get the fuck out of
my sight!"

The three of us quickly exited the duty hut.
I'm not sure which of us was the most stunned, but
the decision had been made and apparently wasn't
open to discussion, so we were left to make the best
of it. It was apparent to the rest of the squad what had
happened when Masters and I traded racks, as I was
now located at the head of the squad bay and Masters
was in the rear. A few of the recruits in the squad

offered a word or two of encouragement to me, but the rest remained silent, not knowing what to think about it. As tempting as it was to tell Masters that he'd better not be a fuck up, I resisted the urge. I figured he had been humiliated enough for one day.

The next day was our last training day of the first phase, and another surprise awaited me. As we were gathered in the squad bay listening to our drill instructor explain what would be taking place the following day as we moved out of the barracks and prepared to be transported to the rifle range at Camp Pendleton, two new recruits entered the barracks and reported for duty. They were my two friends from MRP that had just been cleared to return to duty. They got assigned to a squad other than mine and stowed their gear. That evening during free time, I had a chance to touch bases with them. They were as glad to see me as I was to see them. I made sure to tell their squad leader that these guys were not fuck ups so they would be made to feel welcome. I went to sleep that night feeling pretty good about things. I was back in the training cycle, my hand was starting to feel normal, I had been made a squad leader, and now my two best friends from MRP had joined my platoon. It had been an eventful few days.

Chapter 9. The Rifle Range

When we returned from morning chow on moving day, we packed up our gear and marched to a staging area where our gear was loaded onto trucks and we boarded buses that would transport us up Interstate 5 to Camp Pendleton. It was about a forty five minute ride and the time passed quickly. As we ran off the buses and picked up our gear, we were directed to a nearby barracks where we stowed our gear and made up our racks. We were then informed that we would be doing our week of mess duty prior to beginning our rifle range training. We were taken to the mess hall and given our assignments for the following morning and the week to follow. The week of mess duty involved getting up extremely early every morning and reporting for work at the mess hall well before the sun came up. The work was not difficult, but it was very boring and time seemed to pass at an extremely slow pace. By the end of the week, we were all anxious to get on with the rifle training. We did not want to enter a mess hall again for any reason other than to eat there.

The rifle training was to take two weeks. The first week was called snapping in. We did no live firing during snapping in week. We spent hour after hour and day after day learning and then practicing the proper firing positions. We learned how to use the rifle strap to assist us in creating a "tight" position with the rifle. We learned how to assume the prone position, the sitting position, and the standing position. We learned how to sight in on a target and how to "squeeze" the trigger. We spent hours in each position as our range instructors moved around adjusting our positions and tightening us up where necessary. We actually had to stretch and train our muscles to stay in the proper position for long periods of time. It was difficult the first couple of days, but by the end of the week the shooting positions were becoming second nature for us. We learned the "BRASS" system and practiced it endlessly. BRASS stood for breathe, relax, aim, slack, squeeze. We were to take a breath and let it out, consciously relax our body and mind, aim in on the target, slowly pull up the slack in the trigger, and then gently squeeze the trigger until the rifle fired. We were told that when done properly, it should actually surprise us when the rifle fired.

Since I had not fired anything more than a "BB gun" prior to joining the Marines, I was totally focused on what they were teaching us. Some of the other recruits had grown up around guns and had been firing rifles since they were five years old. They were extremely confident that they would excel on the range. I had no idea what to expect, so I figured I'd better master what they were teaching us in order to develop enough skill to qualify on the range. We were told we could qualify as a marksman, a sharp shooter, or a rifle expert depending on our total score on qualification day. To shoot less than a marksman meant you were "unqualified" or "unk" as it was called. It was made very clear to us that you did not want to go "unk" on the range.

Our week of snapping in finally ended and we

marched to the range for our first day of live firing. The range master spent a great deal of time that first morning explaining the rules of the range and how important it was to practice range safety and to obey all commands given by range personnel. We had already spent many hours getting intimately familiar with our rifles, breaking them down, reassembling them, and cleaning them endlessly. Now we were about to use them for the purpose for which they were intended. I was as nervous as I was excited, but focused on everything they had shown us during our snapping in week. We were all given a small log in which to document each and every shot we took in order to help us set up the "dope" on our rifles for qualification day. The "dope" was what we called the adjustment settings on the rifle for elevation and

215

windage. The idea was to fire your weapon exactly the same each time so that your rounds would strike the target in a tight "group" of bullet holes. If your group was too high or too low in relation to the bulls-eye, you would adjust your elevation setting on the sights accordingly until your group landed in the bulls-eye. If your group was to the left or right of the bulls-eye, you would adjust the windage setting on the sights accordingly.

We fired from the standing position at the 200 yard line, from the sitting and prone positions at the 300 yard line, and from the prone position only at the 500 yard line. The commands from the range master were given over a loud speaker and were very clear. The targets were down below a protective berm in the area referred to as "the butts" and would only rise into

216

view on the verbal command of the range master. The series of commands went like this: "**All ready on the left.........all ready on the right.......the firing line is ready. Shooters, watch your targets.......targets!**" At that time the targets would be raised up into view by the recruits manning the butts and firing could commence. At the end of the firing exercise, the range master would bellow out the command to "**Cease fire......cease fire!**" and the targets would disappear below the berm. The recruits there would mark the bullet holes with small colored discs so the shooters would be able to see where they hit the target and then they would roll the target back up into view for the shooters to chart their shots. If a shooter missed the target entirely, instead of the colored discs, the target would come back up clean and a flag would be

217

waved back and forth slowly across the front of the target. This was referred to as getting "Maggie's drawers" and whoever Maggie was........you never wanted to see her drawers come up in front of your target.

As I began firing, I concentrated on maintaining a proper position and practicing the BRASS system as instructed. By using the techniques taught to us during the snapping in week, I found that I could fire my rounds in a pretty tight group. Then it became a matter of adjusting the elevation and/or the windage by a click or two to move my group closer to the bulls-eye. By the end of our first day of live firing, I was striking the bulls-eye with the majority of my shots. My confidence was soaring when we left the range that day.

The next two days were spent firing again and again from the different positions and distances, charting every shot and continuing to adjust our "dope" until we were sure it was just right. We took our turns working the butts area as well. It was quite an experience being in the butts. As the rounds came whistling overhead they would strike the target with a loud "smack" and then you could see the rounds raise up puffs of dirt as they went through the target and hit the dirt embankment in the back. You felt good when you were able to mark shots in or around the bulls-eye, but felt awful when you occasionally had to wave Maggie's drawers after a missed shot. You knew some poor recruit was hearing it from their drill instructor and range coach whenever that would happen.

For me, the toughest position to fire from was the standing position. Because the "kick" from the 7.62 mm round being fired from the M-14 was substantial, each shot required you to readjust yourself and settle into a new stance before your next shot. And as hard as I tried to hold the rifle steady through the whole BRASS method, it did tend to move around a bit just from the sheer weight of the rifle. My groups weren't as tight from the standing position as they were from the sitting or prone positions. In those positions, you could get yourself into such a tight position that when the rifle "kicked" back into your shoulder, your body would rock right back into the position you started at and you were ready to fire again immediately. Being locked into a tight position was vital during the timed "rapid" fire exercises.

I found that I could hold my own at the 200 yard line in the standing position in relation to how everyone else was firing........we all struggled a bit in that mode. But I excelled from the 300 yard line in the sitting and prone positions, rarely missing the bulls-eye. And I was equally at home in the prone position from the 500 yard line, which surprised me a bit because I could barely even see the bulls-eye. The fact that I could hit it consistently from that distance just validated the shooting technique I had been instructed in.

Because I had never fired a rifle before, I only knew how to fire one the way I was instructed to there in boot camp. I had no bad habits to overcome. Those recruits that had grown up firing rifles had developed

221

habits that now got in the way of what they were trying to accomplish. It was actually working to my advantage that I was inexperienced in shooting, much to my surprise, and theirs. After returning to the barracks area from the range, we spent a good deal of time cleaning our rifles and making sure they were ready for the following day. As a squad leader, I was assigned a squad box that contained all the cleaning equipment needed for my squad members to properly care for their rifles. We would sit together near the squad box and compare notes as we cleaned and oiled our weapons. As we approached "pre-qual" day, the first day that we would follow the qualification routine to the letter and track our scores before firing for qualification purposes the following day, I noticed that while my confidence was growing, there were others who were extremely nervous and fearful of going "unk" on qualification day. I just kept repeating to them to use the BRASS system exactly as they taught us.......that was what I was doing and it worked to great effect. I could understand why some feared what was to come, because the drill instructors had really "lightened up" the manner in which they treated us during this week of live firing. That would all change for those that did not score well on the range. While some dreaded what they might or might not score on pre-qual day, I looked forward to it. I felt I would shoot a qualifying score for sure, and had a good chance to fire expert if all went well.

When pre-qual day finally arrived, the conditions were perfect. It was a cool morning, but the sun was out and there was no wind to have to take into account as we checked our rifles, loaded our magazines and prepared to fire for score for the first time. To fire "expert" a score of 220 points was necessary.

I adjusted the sights of my rifle according to the "dope" I had determined in our many practice sessions. We fired first from the 200 yard line in the standing position. My results in that set were much as they had been during the practice sessions, good but not great. I wasn't concerned because I knew my strength was at the 300 yard line from the sitting and prone positions. That was where I expected to score the bulk of my points.

In preparation for the "rapid fire" line from the sitting position, I tightened the rifle strap around my left arm and settled into an extremely tight position. The tightness of your position was vital to your success in the rapid fire segment, as the kick from each round would rock you back. If your position was tight enough, your rifle would rock right back into the proper firing position so that you were ready to squeeze off the next round immediately and didn't have to use valuable time to readjust your aim on the target. I had been extremely effective in this exercise during the practice rounds and I was totally focused when the range master announced the firing line was ready and had the targets raised.

My mind repeated the BRASS steps over and over as I squeezed off each round. After each round, I rocked right back into the proper firing position and the bulls-eye lined right up at the tip of my sights. As I fired off the final round in my magazine well within

225

the allotted time frame, I couldn't wait to see the result.

The targets went down to be marked and scored, and then were raised to show the shooters how they scored. I was excited to see that I had fired an extremely tight "group" and my group of shots had all landed within the bulls-eye. I had scored the maximum points possible in the rapid fire segment. I knew that if I fired the rest of the segments as, or nearly as, effective as I had during practice, I would post a very good score and may even reach the goal of 220 points to achieve expert status. I remained totally focused through each and every shot. I repeated breathe, relax, aim, slack, and squeeze to myself over and over again as I prepared to fire each round. When I had finished firing from the prone position at the

500 yard line, it was time to total up my score.

The range coach that has served as my "spotter" totaled up my points and gave me the news.

"You just fired a 226 private.........out fucking standing!"

Expert........I had just recorded a score of expert on pre-qual day! I was excited beyond words, and very confident that I could repeat the performance the next day for our final qualification firing. I felt like I was walking on air as we marched back to the barracks that afternoon. Cleaning my rifle was not a chore on this day, it was an absolute pleasure.

That evening, the drill instructor on duty reported out how we had all done. There were several of us that had fired expert, with my score being the second highest of the day. The drill instructor couldn't praise us enough for our efforts. There were several that had scored just below expert at the sharpshooter level, and he praised their efforts as well. The largest group had fired at the marksman level and he told them they needed more focus and a better effort the following morning. Then there were a few hapless recruits who had trouble on the range and had not fired well enough to qualify. While the rest of us got extra "free time" that evening, these poor recruits spent some "up close and personal" time with the drill instructor in the duty hut. He ensured they were "motivated" to do better on the range the next day. When they finally came out of the duty hut, they were wide-eyed and looked like they fully expected their lives to end if they did not qualify the next morning. I was thankful that I had experienced success on the range and didn't fall into that group. I felt sorry for those that had gone "unk" as some of them were doing really well in all other areas of the training. Qualification day would be stressful enough for the rest of us, but for those that had gone "unk" on pre-qual day, the pressure was almost too much to bear as evidenced by the "deer in the headlights" look on their faces after their motivation session in the duty hut.

On qualification day, the conditions were once again ideal. It was a cool, clear morning with no noticeable breeze to factor in. Our range coaches were at the ready to look through their scopes and record our scores as we went through the progression of firing from the standing, sitting, and prone positions from the various distances. Our drill instructor was pacing around like an expectant father waiting for word on his first child. I was confident in the shooting skills I had developed, but still felt an uncomfortable knot in my stomach due to the gravity of the moment. It was drummed into us that every Marine is a rifleman first and foremost, and anything else you were measured on paled in comparison to how you do on the range.

I mentally went through the BRASS progression, breathe, relax, aim, slack, squeeze on every single shot as I fired from the standing position at the 200 yard line to begin qualifying. My score from that position and distance was in line with what I had recorded on pre-qual day, so I felt good going into the other positions and felt confident I would be able to duplicate my score from the previous day. As I prepared for the sitting "rapid fire" segment, I knew how important it was to assume a tight position so that after each shot I would rock right back into a proper position to fire the next shot immediately. I felt I had a good position when I fired the first round upon the command, but when I rocked back into position, the sight was not aligned properly on the bulls-eye. I had to adjust and aim in again after each shot, which consumed valuable time and caused me to rush through the critical "slack and squeeze" part of my firing technique so as to get all rounds fired in the allotted period of time. While I succeeded in getting all rounds fired before time expired, I fell short of scoring the maximum points available as I had done on my pre-qual score. My score was good, but not what I was capable of from this position. I knew there was precious little room for error in the remaining firing segments if I was to qualify as an expert. I concentrated on each and every shot I still had available to me and scored well leading up to the final segment which consisted of firing ten rounds from the prone position at the 500 yard line. According to my range coach, I would need all ten rounds to strike the bulls-eye in order to reach the goal of 220 points and an expert rating. The first six or seven rounds were shown to have hit the bulls-eye, but then two of my remaining rounds appeared to be marked in the ring just outside the bulls-eye. I felt like I had been kicked in the gut as the coach told me I had shot 218, a good score and a rating of sharpshooter, but short of my goal of expert. I dreaded what the drill instructor would have to say to those who fired lower scores than the day before. I suspected it would not be of a complimentary nature. The coach did tell me that this was the "unofficial" score and the "official" score would be recorded by those in the butts area. Those scores sometimes varied either up or down by a few points, as those who marked the targets were able to determine exactly where each round landed as opposed to the range coaches who sometimes couldn't be sure how a specific round had been marked on the target. I held out hope that maybe the butts score would get me to the threshold of 220 points. Unfortunately, we wouldn't receive the official scores for several days, after we had returned to the recruit depot for our final phase of training.

That afternoon, we returned to our barracks

233

area and prepared for our move back to the recruit depot. We spent some time on the concrete area in front of the barracks meticulously cleaning our rifles after the live firing we had just completed. I had just finished with my rifle when the drill instructor came over and informed me I needed to go to a nearby office building and sign some paperwork in my enlistment packet that had somehow been overlooked. The rest of my squad members were still working on their rifles, so I left the squad box with the cleaning materials there, secured my rifle in the barracks rifle rack, and reported to the building I had been directed to for the signing of some paperwork. I hadn't been gone long, no more than twenty minutes or so, but when I returned, the platoon was no longer on the concrete cleaning their rifles. I entered the barracks and immediately asked one of my squad members where the squad box was. He told me the drill instructor had it. Just then, the guide saw me and came over to tell me the drill instructor wanted to see me as soon as I returned. I approached the door of the duty hut with a huge knot in my stomach, knowing that whatever was about to happen was not going to be pleasant.

Our platoon commander had been with us at the range for our qualification firing, but he had now left the area and the drill instructor on duty with us was the most junior of the three. In fact, he had only come to our platoon on the day we left the recruit depot and made the trip to Camp Pendleton for the rifle range phase of our training. One of the original drill instructors for our platoon had received orders to

Viet Nam and had taken leave prior to his shipping out date. He was replaced by the drill instructor I was to meet with, who had just completed drill instructor's school and was still developing his "style" of leadership. We didn't know quite what to make of this relatively young instructor yet. We didn't have a lot of interaction with him while we were on mess duty and then learning how to fire our weapons. He was an unknown quantity to us at this point in time, but I was about to get to know him on a very personal level.

Bang, bang, bang I knocked on the duty hut door.

"Sir, Private Andrews requests permission to enter the duty hut, Sir!" I screamed.

After banging on the door and screaming out

my request two more times, because I apparently sounded like a mouse at the door, the drill instructor finally allowed me to enter.

"Get in here!" he bellowed.

I ran into the duty hut and assumed the position of attention in front of the drill instructors desk. I noted that he already had a scowl on his face, and the squad box was prominently displayed on the desk in front of him,

"Sir, Private Andrews reporting as ordered, sir!" I barked out in a loud voice.

The drill instructor eyed me up and down with a look of disgust on his face. To coin a phrase, I knew I was up a creek and there was no paddle in sight. He made me sweat it out for a minute or two before he spoke.

"Private Andrews........are you responsible for this squad box?"

"Sir, yes sir!" I responded.

"Well if you are responsible for it, then why was it left outside and not secured properly when your squad finished cleaning their weapons?" he asked.

"Sir, the private was ordered to report to another location and was not present when the squad finished cleaning their weapons, sir!"

This, of course, was information the drill instructor was already aware of. It made little or no difference to him as he pressed the issue.

"I don't give a shit where you were sent," he replied. "I only care that this squad box was left in an unsecured area, and you are the private that is responsible for it. Isn't that true Private Andrews?

Aren't you the private that is responsible for this squad box?"

"Sir, yes sir!

He stood up and came around to the front of his desk, squad box in hand. He stood directly in front of me, eyes bulging and looking at me in an extremely menacing way.

"The point is, Private Andrews that you fucked up by not ensuring this squad box was secured!" he growled at me in a loud and gruff tone of voice. As he said this, he raised the squad box and jabbed it toward my face as though he was going to punch me with it. He stopped short of my face, but got close enough that it caused me to flinch. This was a mistake on my part.

"Oooooooooh........you think I'm stupid

enough to hit you in the face with a squad box? Is that what you think Private Andrews?" he asked sarcastically.

"Sir, no sir!" I responded, knowing I was going to be taken down a trail of questions to which there were no right answers.

"Then why did you flinch private?"

"The private doesn't know sir!" I replied.

"Ooooooh.......the private doesn't know. Well either the private thinks I'm stupid, or the private flinched for no fucking reason. Which is it private?" he asked.

While he was speaking to me, he started bumping the squad box against my chest. Although it wasn't hard enough to injure me, it was hard enough to get my attention. I concentrated on not flinching during this experience. I just looked directly ahead and took it as the conversation progressed.

"Sir, the private doesn't know why he flinched, sir! The private knows the drill instructor is not stupid, sir!"

"Well Private Andrews, the fact of the matter is that you are responsible for this squad box and it was left unsecured. What should we do about that?" he asked, seeming to be enjoying himself at this point. He continued bumping my chest with the squad box.

"Sir, the private doesn't know, sir!" I answered.

"Well I know what to do Private Andrews," he said in a firm tone. He finally stopped bumping me with the squad box, leaving my chest very tender and sore. "Since you can't be trusted to carry out your

241

responsibilities, I don't think you should have any. You are fired as a squad leader. Now get the fuck out of here, and send in the guide and Private Masters!"

"Sir, aye aye, sir!" I answered, relieved that the session was ending. I did an about face and left the duty hut as quickly as I could.

I informed the guide and Private Masters that the drill instructor wanted to see them and watched as they entered the duty hut where Private Masters was again hired as a squad leader.

That evening, those that had reportedly fired expert were celebrated by the drill instructor and given extra free time. Those few that had failed to qualify were treated to an extra "motivational" session, from which they returned red faced, huffing and puffing, and with a tear or two running down more than one cheek. The rest of us were tasked with giving the barracks a good cleaning since we were departing for the recruit depot the next morning. I suffered the double humiliation of not qualifying as an expert, and then losing my job as a squad leader. Still, I was glad to be returning to the recruit depot for our final phase of training. The end was in sight!

Chapter 10. Final phase

Upon our return to the recruit depot, we found ourselves assigned back to the same barracks we had previously occupied. This time, however, we were assigned to the second floor of the building which meant we would have some stairs to navigate every time we entered or left the barracks. We didn't care though, we were just happy to be back from the range and starting our final phase of training.

Our first night back, the drill instructor on duty called for us to gather by the duty hut and then informed us the final scores from the rifle range were in already. As he called out each recruits name, he called out the score and what shooting badge that score rated. There were some slight changes in several of the scores that had been reported to us on qualification night at the range. Some were adjusted to a lower score, and others to a higher score. Some mattered little, as the new score was still in the same range as the original score for a shooting badge. But there were a few significant changes that moved a recruit into a higher or lower range and changed which shooting badge they were to receive. My own prayers were answered when I learned that instead of qualifying as a sharpshooter, my final score was adjusted up by two points and I had actually qualified as a rifle expert. I felt a tremendous pride when I heard my new score called out, but at the same time, I felt like I had been cheated out of the special treatment "experts" received on our final night at the range. Likewise, there was one recruit who had been included in the "experts" group at the range who now learned that he had been dropped into the sharpshooter category. There was one other change that was of special significance to me. Private Masters, who had been rehired as our squad leader when I was fired, had just barely qualified as a marksman at the range. He now learned that he had actually gone "unk", or unqualified. He would be among those few who were relieved they had not been dropped from training because of their low score, but he would suffer the humiliation of not having a shooting badge displayed on his uniform at graduation.

While Masters continued in the role of a squad leader, his confidence had been visibly shaken and he had little to say to anyone in his squad after that. By now though, we all knew what was expected of us and it wasn't really necessary for him to ride herd on the squad anymore. He became somewhat of a "squad leader in name only" for the final phase.

There were several changes that took place in the final phase that served to identify us as a final phase platoon. Just as we were pleased to trade our tennis shoes for combat boots during the first phase of training, we were now even more pleased to be able to "blouse" our boots in the final phase. Our utility trousers had been worn over the top of our boots in phase one and at the rifle range. We were now allowed to place thin springs, designed for this purpose, around the top portion of our boots and tuck our trouser legs around the springs, exposing the full boot. This clearly identified us as a platoon nearing graduation and we bloused our boots with great pride. With each passing day, we were beginning to look more and more like Marines rather than scared recruits. We were allowed to keep just a hint of hair on the top of our heads at our visits to the barber shop, having just the sides shaved giving us the "high and tight" look rather than the "all skin" look of a new recruit. When we went out for physical fitness training, we left our caps off to allow the top of our heads to get some sun. Our caps were always on during first phase, which created a distinctive look as the lower half our heads became tanned, while the upper half remained extremely white. We were very happy to have a bit of hair, slight as it was, and some color on our heads. We eventually starched out utility caps and our utility shirts and trousers, giving us the look of a truly "squared away" platoon of Marines. Our marching, as we moved around on the base, was now nearly perfect. I recalled how I had seen a platoon go by in the early days of our training that looked so good that I couldn't believe that we would ever match them. Now, I could tell that first phase platoons looked at us with that same awe as we marched by. The transition from where we were in phase one to where we were now was nothing short of remarkable.

Throughout the final phase we trained hard, with a focus on those areas we would be scored on such as physical fitness, the obstacle course, drill movements, and our knowledge of Marine Corps history and traditions.

We took very few trips to the "pit" in final

phase, so our physical fitness training was of the more organized variety. Our "PT" uniforms consisted of a tee shirt, shorts, white socks, and tennis shoes. Our "PT" sessions consisted of push-ups, pull-ups, sit-ups, and of course everyone's favorite......bends and motherfuckers. By now, we had done so many repetitions of these exercises that we literally felt like we could do them forever if ordered to do so. When it came to running, we sometimes went on platoon runs in our "PT" gear, but at other times we ran in our combat boots, utility trousers, and tee shirts. Our platoon runs during first phase were almost torturous in nature, with some recruits lagging behind and virtually all of us fighting through side aches and gasping for air. But now we were working into top condition and our platoon runs were something many of us actually looked forward to. We ran in formation at a steady pace, with our boots all hitting the ground beneath us in unison. We looked and sounded like a well-oiled machine as we easily covered the three miles we would be tested on prior to graduation. Instead of having to drop back and holler at stragglers, our drill instructors now ran beside the platoon singing out various chants that we would repeat back to them in unison. The chants were very motivating, and along with the sound of the boots striking the ground, helped keep our minds off the physical effort we were putting our bodies through on these runs.

We also got plenty of practice running through the obstacle course in final phase. This was something we knew we would be tested on as well. Early in first phase, it had been quite a challenge getting over, under, and through the various obstacles at all, let alone in a timely fashion. But now, we were able to navigate through the course in short order. Obstacles that had seemed almost insurmountable in phase one were now little more than a nuisance as we made our way through the course. Our drill instructors, who had spent their time in first phase hollering, swearing, and threatening physical harm to motivate us to get over the wall or up the rope, now used stop watches to time us on the various obstacles and seemed quite pleased at how we were doing. We often heard our favorite phrase as they clicked their stop watches on and off.

"Out......fucking.....standing!" It was sweet music to our ears because we knew we wouldn't be making a stop at the "pit" afterwards.

We continued with many classroom sessions in final phase, learning the history and traditions of the Corps, learning first aid techniques, learning our general orders (which we would be called on to recite at any given moment), and practicing breaking down and reassembling our rifles as well as memorizing all the characteristics of our weapon. We carried small notebooks in our back pockets containing everything we were required to memorize, and anytime we were standing in line at the chow hall, or waiting in a classroom for instruction to begin, we would "break out our knowledge" and study. There were no wasted minutes in final phase. We were either actively participating in a training exercise, or studying our knowledge.

And while we could now move around the base, perfectly performing basic marching maneuvers, we were instructed in more intricate drill movements and we practiced them for hours on end to prepare for our final drill evaluation. We had progressed from an unruly mob that couldn't even step off with the same foot at the same time, to a group that now performed precise movements in perfect unison. The hours spent on the parade deck were long and tedious, but we were totally focused on getting it right. We knew our hard work would pay off when we were evaluated at our "final drill" exercise.

We had taken notice of platoons ready for graduation who had several ribbon-like streamers hanging from their guide-on. We knew we would have the opportunity to earn some of those streamers and worked hard to ensure that we did. We had already completed the rifle range, so we knew we had already won that streamer or not, depending on how the other platoons in our series had scored. But all the other streamers were still in play. The final drill, final inspection, practical exam, physical readiness test, obstacle course, and written exam were all out there to be won and we wanted to win our share.

Our evenings were spent preparing our gear and our uniforms for final inspection, and studying our knowledge. We worked and worked on "spit polishing" our leather, and used "Dura-Glit" and "Brasso" to break down and shine our brass (belt buckles). Our uniforms were tailored to fit us perfectly and had to be meticulous for inspection. We removed any hint of lint from our wool dress uniforms with scotch tape, and searched for and eliminated any loose threads that might appear. These threads were called "Irish pennants" and were not removed by pulling them or cutting them. They were removed by using a lighter to burn them off. I'm not sure how the Irish came to be blamed for loose threads, I only knew that none of them could be left in view for an inspector to find.

Our days were so full, from before the sun came up to well after it went down, that the time passed very quickly in final phase and we soon found ourselves beginning the final tests and examinations.

Our written exam contained no surprises or trick questions. We had spent so much time studying our "knowledge" that the answers to the questions came easily and quickly. We knew the rank structure, the history and traditions of the Marine Corps, and the general orders as well as we knew our own names. We were all extremely confident we had performed well as individuals and as a platoon in this exam.

For the practical exam, each recruit in turn went from station to station demonstrating the various skills we had learned. At one station, the recruit was seated at a table with an M-14 rifle laying on it. The recruit was blindfolded and then given a short amount of time to disassemble and then reassemble the rifle. We had done this process so many times that doing so blindfolded was no challenge at all......I think we could have done it in our sleep. At another station, we were asked to demonstrate how to use various items as a splint, how to apply a compress bandage, and how to treat a sucking chest wound. At still another

257

station, we were asked to demonstrate the various

bayonet fighting techniques such as the thrust, the

parry, and the horizontal butt stroke. All of these

things came easy to us, as we had these things drilled

into us to the point that we were able to perform them

without even thinking.......acting on instinct alone

was sufficient. All of our work, all the repetitions, all

of the being pushed by our drill instructors beyond

what we thought were our limits, was beginning to

pay off.

When the time came to take the "Commandant

of the Marine Corps Readiness Test", a test of our

physical strength and conditioning, we were

extremely confident. To a man, we were in the best

physical condition of our lives. All of those exercises

we had done on a daily basis, all of the running we

had done, and yes, even all of our trips to the "pit" doing bends and motherfuckers in first phase, had combined to mold us into impressive physical specimens. That's not to say that we had bulging muscles like you would see on a weight lifter. On the contrary......we were lean and mean. We had good muscle definition, but it was a more streamlined and functional look than if we had just "bulked" up. We had "washboard" abs, broad shoulders, and narrow hips. There was no doubt we would pass this test.......it was only a question of how high could we score?

We shouted encouragement to each other as we each took our turns performing on the pull up bar and cranking out as many sit ups as we could in a two minute period. I was able to get maximum points on the pull up bar, but when it came to the sit ups I just couldn't get 80 of them done in two minutes to score the maximum points. As I had in every practice session, I got in 70 in quick order but then "hit the wall" and each sit up after 70 was a struggle for me and time was called before I could reach 80. Still, it was a high score and set me up to pass the overall test with flying colors. The three mile timed run would not be a problem.

Although we were to be timed and scored as individuals in the run, we were focused on doing well as a platoon too. We wanted that streamer on our guide-on. To get it, we had to ensure that everyone passed, and that everyone got the best time they possibly could. As we progressed through the run, we started to string it out a bit, as some were moving along almost effortlessly, but others were slowing down and having to work at it. As we made the final turn on the course and could see the finish line ahead of us, those of us that were out ahead of the rest knew we had plenty of time to complete the run and we would have a chance to get maximum points in the process. But it was more important to us that we all did well as a platoon, so several of us dropped back to shout encouragement and run with those that were slowing down to help them finish the run in decent time. We sacrificed our own personal time (knowing that we would still pass and score well) in an effort to help the slower runners in the platoon, and it paid off. Everyone passed, and everyone scored more than the minimum required points on the run. Our effort did not go unnoticed by our drill instructors who were proud to see us working as a team and shouted out a hearty **"Out…..fucking…..standing!"** as we crossed the finish line.

Our guide-on began to accumulate streamers that had been awarded to us for the various scored training exercises. As we would arrive at classes and/or training areas at the same time as the other three platoons in our series, it was evident that we had won our share as compared to the other platoons. One platoon had yet to win a streamer and their guide-on looked bare compared to the other platoons. I felt sorry for them, as I'm sure they continued to suffer the wrath of their drill instructors for not performing at an acceptable level. I was thankful that I had not been assigned to that platoon when I came out of the Medical Rehabilitation Platoon. The two biggest tests we would face still remained. We would be evaluated and scored on our drill capabilities, and our last and most important test would be the final inspection.

When we learned which drill instructor would take us through the paces in our final drill evaluation, we were quite pleased by the selection. The drill instructor assigned was the one we related to the best as we marched and performed the various maneuvers. He had a calm way about him and called out the orders in a clear and concise manner. There was never any confusion about what we were being ordered to do. We always performed at our best level when he took us out for drill practice and we felt confident in our ability to score well on final drill with this particular drill instructor in the lead.

After countless hours of practice, the morning

finally came when we were to perform in our final drill evaluation. Our utilities were freshly starched and pressed, our brass gleamed, and our boots were polished to a fine gloss. Our M-14 rifles were clean and gleaming as well. When we formed up for the march to the parade deck, we looked good and we knew it. We were brimming with confidence, and although I think we all had a small knot in our stomachs from the realization of how important this was, we knew we were ready and couldn't wait to get at it. Our drill instructor was dressed in his full class "A" uniform and he looked impeccable. He had a sword strapped to his side, which was not something we had seen before. He gave us the order to march and led us out to the parade deck where we would be evaluated. He brought us to a halt and we waited at parade rest for the evaluation team to arrive.

In short order, an officer arrived, accompanied by two senior staff NCO's carrying clip boards. Our drill instructor ordered the platoon to attention. He then drew his sword and went into a formal "present arms" position with it. With his sword gleaming in the morning sunlight, the drill instructor presented our platoon for final drill evaluation. The officer saluted, and then ordered our drill instructor to carry on.

He raised his sword from the present arms position and rested it against shoulder much like a rifle. He did an about face and surveyed the platoon. He looked confident, and all business. I thought I detected a slight nod, as if to say "You're ready.......let's do this!"

Before marching, he put us through a series of

rifle movements. **"Present......arms!"**

"Order......arms!" "Right shoulder.....arms!"

"Left shoulder......arms!" "Order.....arms!"

Our movements were precise and completely in unison. We had done these actions so many times that they were automatic for us. He then took us out onto the parade deck and put us through all of the marching maneuvers we had been instructed in under the watchful eyes of the evaluation team, who were making a lot of notations on their clip boards. We completed each and every maneuver with no apparent flaws. As a group, we had all brought our "A" games and were performing to the very best of our abilities. Our drill instructor was precise in his commands and his movements (he was being scored as well), and the manner in which he handled his sword was just the coolest thing I had ever seen. When we had completed our final drill evaluation, we stood at attention and waited for the officer in charge of the evaluation team to dismiss us. Our drill instructor saluted with a sword movement and the officer returned a hand salute while verbally dismissing the platoon.......officially ending our final drill evaluation.

As our drill instructor did an about face, he looked us over for a moment before giving the command to march us off the parade deck. He had an 'ever so slight' hint of a smile on his face, and gave us a distinct nod of approval. Our chests were puffed out and we were almost walking on air as we returned to the barracks area. We had nailed it.......and we knew it.

Before he dismissed the platoon, the drill instructor gave us a loud and resounding

"Out.........fucking.........standing!"

We now had one last test before graduation.......our final inspection. At final inspection, we would be judged not just on our uniforms and appearance, but also on our overall military bearing, the cleanliness of our rifles, and our military knowledge.

We devoted more and more time in the evenings to making sure our brass was shined, our shoes were "spit shined" to a high gloss, and that no Irish pennants could be found anywhere on our uniform items. We also continued to study our "knowledge" so that we would be prepared to answer any and all questions we might be asked by the inspecting officer.

Whichever drill instructor was on duty in the evenings seemed to be more at ease as graduation day approached. Instead of the constant yelling, name calling, and general harassment we had become accustomed to in first phase, they now spoke to us in a civil manner most of the time. They spent some time explaining to us what would be taking place in the last few days, what would happen on graduation day, and what to expect afterwards. They didn't refer to us as Marines yet.......but at least we weren't made to feel like we were the scum of the earth anymore.

Our platoon commander had received orders to Viet Nam during the course of our final phase and we were informed he wouldn't be with us as we graduated. In fact, we wouldn't see him at all in the last few days. His final night with the platoon, he spoke to us telling us how proud he was of us and how he hoped to serve with us one day in the fleet. He wasn't all warm and fuzzy with us, but he spoke to us with a degree of respect that we not experienced before this night. When we said our prayers that night, we included him in there......right after Chesty.

One night, a few days prior to graduation, it was announced who the meritorious promotions to PFC (private first class) would be. Those promotions traditionally went to the platoon guide and the squad leaders. They announced them ahead of time because the recipients needed to send their graduation day uniforms to the tailor shop to have the single stripe designating the rank of PFC sewn onto the shirt sleeves and the outer blouse sleeves.

Having been fired as a squad leader, I was certainly not expecting my name to be called with the others being promoted. One by one, the drill instructor on duty called out the names of the guide and the squad leaders.......until it came to our squad. Much to my surprise, and that of Private Masters I'm sure, my name was called out instead of his. I wasn't sure what had just happened, or why, but I certainly wasn't going to question it. Afterwards, when everyone else turned to on getting their gear ready for final inspection, I was called to the duty hut.

After the usual banging on the door and screaming at the top of my lungs to gain entrance, the drill instructor on duty that night explained the promotion decision to me. This was not the drill instructor who had fired me, and I was thankful he hadn't been on duty that night. I'm sure the conversation would have had a different tone to it had he been the one to tell me.

"Private Andrews.......I'm sure you're wondering why you are getting the promotion instead of Private Masters," he started.

"Sir, yes sir," I replied.

"The platoon commander is the one that appointed you to squad leader......and he didn't agree with the drill instructor on duty at the range who fired you. He didn't want to override the decision of one of his staff, so he let that stand. But before he left, he submitted the names for promotion and felt you had earned the promotion over Masters, especially after Masters went "unk" on the range and you shot expert. So Masters is still the squad leader, but you get the meritorious promotion. So congratulations........now get out of here!"

"Sir, aye aye sir!" I responded.

I later saw Private Masters going to the duty hut, undoubtedly to get his own explanation of why he wasn't promoted. He seemed upset when he came out, but never said a word to me about it.

We finally reached the night before final inspection was to occur and the barracks was alive with recruits going over all their gear one last time. The drill instructor on duty went from one private to the next looking over everyone's gear to ensure they were ready. There were a few who had shoes that were not as glossy as they needed to be, in spite of several hours of polishing. For whatever reason, they didn't measure up. But instead of getting hard on their case, the drill instructor told them to bring their shoes to the duty hut where he would apply a "magical" substance that would help them pass the inspection. When the privates left the duty hut after having their shoes "enhanced" with the magical substance, their shoes did look remarkably better. We later learned that the magic substance came out of a can of Pledge wax. That little tidbit of information is something we all filed away for future use if necessary. All of our free time that evening was devoted to checking, double checking, and triple checking every stitch of clothing we would be wearing at the inspection, everything that needed to be highly polished, and the cleanliness of our rifles. When we were sure our gear was ready, we turned to on studying our "knowledge" and tried to anticipate what questions we might be asked by the inspecting officer.

The following morning, we dressed out in our utility uniforms and went to morning chow as usual. Upon returning to the barracks area, we were ordered to fall out and prepare for final inspection. After taking the utmost care in donning our dress uniforms, and making sure not to smudge the shine on our shoes or our brass, we looked each over with a critical eye searching for any stray "Irish pennants" that may have magically appeared. Everyone checked their rifle for cleanliness one last time and then we fell out into formation in front of the barracks and awaited our fate.

We stood in formation in the parade rest position for what seemed like hours, but was actually only a few minutes. Everyone stood perfectly still, and in the silence there was scant evidence that anyone was even breathing. Finally, we heard the footsteps of the inspectors approaching. Our drill instructor brought us to the position of attention, and then formally presented the platoon for final inspection with a crisp salute to the lead inspecting officer.

As the inspector would step in front of each individual recruit, the recruit would bring his rifle to the position of inspection arms. This maneuver was accomplished with crisp movements bringing the rifle up and then positioned vertically in front of the recruit and held in place with both hands. This was an art form, and one we had practiced many times before this inspection. Your hold on the rifle had to be firm enough that you wouldn't drop it, but loose enough

276

that you could release it the instant the inspecting officer "snapped" it out of your hands to inspect it. Once the inspector made contact with your rifle, you had to release it and drop your hands to your sides in the position of attention so fast it was as if you had never been holding the rifle in the first place. The movement had to be perfect. Letting go too soon might result in the rifle being dropped, and that would result in failing your inspection and would undoubtedly lead to a session with the drill instructor afterwards that would not be fun. If you held it too long, making it difficult for the inspector to take possession of the rifle, the same fate awaited you. It had to be perfect!

While the officer was inspecting your rifle, he would bark out several questions which required instantaneous responses. I could hear many of the questions and responses as the inspector worked his way down the rank I was standing in. I quickly went over a number of details in my head to be ready to respond should I be asked. What was my service number? What was my rifle number? What was the first general order? What was the fifth general order? Who was the Commandant of the Marine Corps? What are the characteristics of the M-14 rifle? How do you stop a sucking chest wound? So many different things could be asked. I heard one recruit answer a question with "The private doesn't know sir!" and I cringed. I prayed that wouldn't happen to me. I literally prayed under my breath......."Please God, let me know the answers to the questions I'm asked......and don't let me cause the rifle to be dropped."

I stood so still, I could have been mistaken for a statue. Finally, the inspecting officer stood face to face with me. In short, quick movements, I came to the position of inspection arms. He shot his right hand out and "slapped" the stock of my rifle, at which time I released and shot my hands down to my side. The timing had to be perfect, and it was. He was quickly looking the rifle over, inspecting the trigger housing assembly, the barrel, and all aspects of the rifle for cleanliness. As he did so, he barked out several questions to me. I responded to each and every question instantaneously in a loud voice and with the correct answer. He held the rifle out for me to claim it and return it to the position of attention. I successfully completed the transfer of the rifle and snapped it back down to my side in the position of attention. The inspector looked me up and down and found nothing to be critical of. He gave me a slight nod, said "Outstanding, Marine!" and then moved on to the next recruit. And there it was.......the first time anyone had actually called me a Marine! The drill instructor followed along at the side of the inspector, and he also gave me a slight nod and I could see just a hint of approval in his eyes even though he was trying hard to remain stone-faced.

The sense of relief that came over me as the inspecting officer moved on down the ranks was huge. This was our last big test prior to graduation, and I had passed it with flying colors. And I had been called a Marine! Since the day we stepped off the bus and onto the yellow footprints, I had been called many things, and none of them were flattering. I had been called a slimy civilian, a girl, a lady, a pussy, a maggot, a worm, a worthless motherfucker, a stupid shit, and countless other things that don't immediately come to mind. But on this day.......I had been called a Marine. That felt unbelievably good........and I thought my chest was about to bust out the front of my uniform I was so proud.

Although there were a few discrepancies found in the process, overall our platoon scored well as a group and our drill instructor was obviously pleased as the inspection team moved on to inspect one of the other platoons in our series. There would be no more trips to the "pit" and there would be no more bends and motherfuckers. All that was left was to prepare for graduation.

Chapter 11.   Night before Graduation

A great deal of time on the night before graduation was spent sitting on the deck in front of the duty hut while our drill instructor talked to us as Marines for the first time. There were no negative references directed toward us, no chewing us out or swearing at us, only a Marine Corps Staff NCO talking to his troops and explaining what was to take place the next day at graduation and immediately thereafter.

We would be getting our gear ready to go and packed into our sea bags for the trip to Camp Pendleton to begin our advanced infantry training. We would be graduating mid-morning and then would be granted four hours of base liberty to spend with the family or friends who would be there to witness our graduation. After our four hours of liberty expired, we would be changing out of the class "A" uniforms we would be wearing at graduation and into utilities and boots for our bus trip to the next phase of our Marine Corps training. We would be part of the Infantry Training Regiment (ITR) for a month and would then be granted a ten day leave prior to reporting to our various military occupational schools.

The drill instructor had a copy of everyone's orders and announced what occupational fields we had all been assigned to. One name after another was followed by some specialty within the infantry field. Rifleman......mortar man........machine gunner.......were called out to all but six of us. They were told that they would get their specialty training

283

after ITR and would be sent through staging and then right to Viet Nam. He congratulated each of them and he shook every man's hand. He told them that they were the backbone of the Marine Corps and it would be his privilege to serve with them in combat on his next tour. Then he told the remaining six, of which I was one, that following ITR we would be reporting to the Naval Air Station in Millington, Tennessee for our various aviation related schools. Millington is a small town on the outskirts of Memphis. He did not congratulate us, or tell us how proud he was of us. He just told us where we would be going and what we would be trained for and left it at that. Until that moment, I had completely forgotten about that whole "aviation guarantee" I was given at the time of enlistment. It had been drummed into us every day of

284

our training that we were training to go to war, and I had worked hard, trained hard, and fully expected to go to war with the rest of the platoon. At that particular moment in time, I felt as though that privilege had been stolen away from me. Most of the platoon would soon be headed to a war zone........I was headed to Memphis. I looked at the other five men who had received orders similar to mine and asked, "Who are we fighting in Memphis?"

After we had been briefed on graduation day and had been told what was to follow in the way of our individual orders, the rest of the evening consisted of the drill instructor telling us what to expect at ITR and then how we should or should not conduct ourselves when we went home on leave.

"Even though you are all in the best physical

condition of your lives, there are two things you should not do when you go home on leave," he counseled us. "You should not make a point of looking up Bobby Bad Ass back on the block……..you know, the guy that used to pick on you…..and challenge him to a fight. If Bobby Bad Ass could beat you up before you left home, there is a chance he might still be able to…..so don't put yourself in that situation."

"On the other hand," he continued……"If Bobby Bad Ass hears you are back from training and comes looking for you……..then stand your ground and do what you've been taught. Chances are, when Bobby sees that you're not afraid of him anymore, he won't push his luck."

"The second thing you should not do is go

286

around strutting your stuff for the ladies back home and jumping into the sack with anyone that smiles at you. You are now the property of the United States Marine Corps and the last thing you or the Marine Corps needs is for you to be out there knocking up the local girls. That's a problem you don't need, so keep it in your pants!"

He then decided to test us......or have a little fun with us, I'm not sure which. He asked if anyone wanted to call their mommy before graduation.

By now, almost all of us had come to the realization that there are no good deals in boot camp and that we should be suspicious of anything purporting to be one. We all sat silent except for one hapless recruit that had not yet learned the lesson.

"Sir, yes sir!" responded one recruit without

having thought it through.

The drill instructor just smiled as he shook his head from side to side.

"Alright private," he said. "Let's go outside and call your mommy."

The recruit followed the drill instructor out of the barracks, where they then stopped on the concrete walkway.

"Go ahead, call her!" bellowed the drill instructor, struggling to keep a straight face.

"Sir?" the recruit responded, now realizing he never should have fallen for this.

"Call her!"

"Mommy," shouted the recruit, knowing for sure now that he had been set up.

"I don't think she can hear you!" said the drill

instructor with a raised voice.

"MOMMY.......MOMMY.......MOMMY!"
shouted the recruit at the top of his lungs until the
drill instructor finally tired of the game. This was
very entertaining to the rest of us, but one last little bit
of humiliation for the victim of this last mind game.

After they came back in, we were told to turn
to on getting our gear ready for the big day tomorrow.
As I went about the business of getting everything
ready, my mind was dwelling on the fact that nearly
everyone else in the platoon was going to Viet Nam,
and I was going to Memphis. It was really eating at
me. I had no interest in going to Memphis.......I had
trained as hard as anyone, and even earned a
meritorious promotion. I wanted to go with the rest of
the platoon to Viet Nam. I thought maybe I could get

289

the aviation guarantee dropped and stay with the platoon as they prepared to go to war. I decided to ask the drill instructor if anything could be done to change my orders.

After banging on the duty hut hatch and being granted permission to enter, I nervously addressed the drill instructor.

"Sir, Private Andrews requests that his orders be changed sir!" I snapped off.

"Private Andrews requests what?" responded the incredulous drill instructor.

"The private requests that his orders be changed, sir!" I repeated. "The private got orders to an aviation school in Memphis, but the private wants to go with the rest of platoon into the infantry and to Viet Nam, sir! The private trained hard and is ready to go to war sir!"

The drill instructor stood up and moved around from the desk he had been seated at, until he stood eye ball to eye ball with me.......no more than a foot away. He reached up his open hand and gave me a good slap across my left cheek. It startled me, but I did not flinch or move a muscle in any way, recalling what happened the last time I flinched.

"You stupid shit!" he barked at me. "Don't you realize how lucky you are? Half of those guys will be coming home in body bags six months from now.......and you'll still be in Memphis! And you think YOU got a raw deal? One thing you're gonna learn about life in the Marine Corps son.......you go where the Marine Corps tells you to go and you do what the Marine Corps tells you to do. The Marine

Corps owns you and they will decide how best to use you. You have no fucking say in it! If the Marine Corps wants you to go to Memphis and learn an aviation skill, then you'll go to Memphis and you'll learn whatever it is they want you to learn! You got that?"

"Sir, yes sir!" I answered.

"Good…….now get the fuck out of here!"

I went back to getting my gear ready with a new perspective on the whole Memphis situation. Maybe it wasn't such a bad deal after all.

That night we said our prayers, still God blessing Chesty Puller and the rest of them, and then closed our eyes and tried to sleep on our last night at Marine Corps Recruit Depot, San Diego. Sleep was slow in coming as my mind raced……replaying everything I had just been through in boot camp, and

thinking ahead, wondering what the Marine Corps

had in store for me. I looked around the darkened

barracks and wondered how accurate the drill

instructors statement about body bags had been.

Would half of these fired up and motivated young

men, in the prime of their lives, really be coming back

in body bags in six months? It was a sobering

thought.

Chapter 12. Graduation

When the lights came on in the barracks on graduation morning, we were all awake, up, and ready to get on with it. When we marched to the chow hall for our last breakfast at MCRD San Diego, we did so with a sense of pride and confidence that only comes with great effort and great achievement. We had taken everything that was thrown at us, and managed to not only survive it but to actually gain strength from and thrive on it. We had made the transition from a scared, undisciplined, and out of shape mob to a physically fit, mentally tough, highly motivated unit of Marines. We looked good as we marched to and from the chow hall that morning and we knew it. Our utility uniforms were starched and crisp, our bloused boots gleamed, and our feet all struck the pavement in perfect unison as we marched along. Our guide-on had numerous streamers dangling proudly, evidence of how well we had performed in the various final phase tests.

It seemed that we were given a little extra time to eat our breakfast that morning, as I was able to eat everything on my tray for the first time since we had stepped off the bus. As we marched back to the barracks, we passed a platoon of brand new, first phase recruits being "herded" toward the chow hall. They were wearing the tell-tale sweat shirts and tennis shoes and looked at us in awe as we passed by.

Back at the barracks, we went about the business of changing out of our utilities and into the class "A" winter service uniform we would be graduating in. We checked over each other carefully, making sure none of those dastardly Irish pennants appeared anywhere.

Before we got into formation for the march to the parade deck in front of the base theater, the drill instructor went over with us what was to take place at the ceremony, and also what would happen afterward. He then moved among us informally, looking each of us over and congratulating us on graduating.

A couple of the recruits from my squad approached me and suggested that since I was the meritorious PFC from our squad, and not the squad leader Masters, that I should lead the squad to the parade deck in his place. I appreciated their thoughts on the subject, but reminded them that Masters had not been relieved of his squad leader responsibilities by the drill instructor. I was sure he felt bad enough as it was, not being a PFC pick along with his fellow squad leaders, and with the added humiliation of not being able to display a shooting award on his uniform. I saw no point in flaunting the fact that I received the promotion rather than him. I had the stripe on my sleeve, and that was good enough for me.

It was finally time, and we marched to a staging area just off the parade deck where we formed up with the other three platoons in our series. We would all be part of the same ceremony and would be graduated together. Even though these other platoons had been our competition during the training cycle, we now felt a kinship with them. We were the fourth platoon in the series and would therefore be the last one to march onto the parade deck. We didn't mind. Our guide-on seemed to have more streamers than any of the other platoons so we felt that demonstrated which one had been the top platoon of the series.

As we marched onto the parade deck for the ceremony, we could see a rather large group of family and friends that had been invited to witness the event and spend time with their graduate during the four hour base liberty that was to follow. I knew that my parents and my girlfriend were somewhere in the crowd and I was anxious to see them. But first things first.

The base commanding officer gave a rather long speech over a loud speaker system, not only congratulating us for our achievement in becoming Marines, but also explaining to the family members what we had just experienced and what it meant to us to now be addressed as United States Marines. He spoke of the history and traditions of the Marine Corps and how we had now taken our place in that long line of honorable and brave men. It was a very inspirational speech, but by the time he wrapped it up we were good and ready to get this over with.

One by one, the three platoons ahead of us were dismissed. Finally the moment we had worked so hard for was upon us. Our drill instructor "presented" our platoon to the commanding officer.......who then ordered him to dismiss us.

The drill instructor turned and faced the platoon, eyes peering out from under the brim of that distinctive and still intimidating "Smokey the Bear" hat.

"**PLATOON 2204**" he bellowed out in a loud and commanding voice, "**DISMISSED!**"

We took one backward step as we had been instructed, shouted out at the top of our lungs an earth shattering "**SIR, PLATOON 2204 IS DISMISSED........AYE AYE SIR!**" ......did an about face, and threw our hats in the air. It was now official......we were no longer "recruits".........we were United States Marines. We swelled with pride as the family members were allowed to come onto the parade deck and find their graduate.

My parents, my younger brother and sister, and my girlfriend all approached me with big smiles on their faces. My mother got the first hug in, followed by my father and siblings, and finally my girlfriend. I took note that although my father had looked at me like I had totally lost my mind when I told my parents I was signing up for the Marines, he now had his chest puffed out there with equal pride to any of the other fathers in attendance.

The four hours of base liberty consisted of access to the post exchange and a family picnic area nearby. We got something to eat and then sat at a picnic table while I spent the next few hours telling them all about the training I had just experienced. I was very careful not to speak in terms they would be shocked to hear me use......terms that had become a daily part of my new "Marine Corps" vocabulary. I didn't realize four hours could pass so quickly, but it was gone in what seemed like the blink of an eye. I explained to everyone that I would be sent up to Camp Pendleton for my advanced infantry training and would then get ten days of "leave" before reporting to Memphis for my aviation school. We could spend some "quality" time then. I said my good byes and watched them leave until they were out of sight. I took a deep breath and let it out slowly, preparing myself for whatever was next in this life changing adventure I had embarked on.

After our guests had all left the area, we formed up our platoon and marched back to the barracks to change into utilities, gather our gear, and prepare to leave for Camp Pendleton.

When the time came, we reported to a staging area with everything we had been issued packed into our sea bags. A truck rolled in and our sea bags were loaded onto it for transport to Camp Pendleton. We then boarded a military bus for the forty five minute ride to Camp Pendleton. As the bus slowly proceeded toward the main gate, we saw another bus, a Greyhound, stopped in a staging area with a bunch of scared recruits running from it and taking positions on yellow footprints. We just smiled and shook our heads as a number of Marines hovered around the group shouting at them and instilling in them a fear like they had never in their short lives experienced. It wasn't hard to remember when that was us......and we were glad those days were now behind us.

We weren't sure what awaited us when we arrived at Camp Pendleton, but we were reasonably sure it wouldn't involve yellow footprints and men screaming at us.

It was an odd feeling as we passed through the main gate and glanced back at the recruit depot. To be sure, we were glad to have graduated and glad we were moving on. But at the same time, we had been put to the test at this place and discovered things about ourselves that couldn't have been learned anywhere else. We would never forget the yellow footprints, or the piercing eyes beneath the rim of the "Smokey the Bear" hats, or our trips to the "pit" where we did "bends and motherfuckers" forever.

As I would tell potential recruits later in my career when I pulled a tour as a Marine Corps recruiter, boot camp is not something you will enjoy, and you would not ever want to do it again, but when it's over, you'll be glad you did it.

Chapter 13.   Camp Pendleton

We were shown to our quarters upon arrival at Camp Pendleton by sergeants that were called "troop handlers"..........there were no yellow footprints and nobody screaming at us at the top of their lungs. Also gone were the "Smokey the Bear" hats. The troop handlers wore utility uniforms, web belts, and helmets. Our quarters were World War II era metal Quonset huts with cement floors. Each hut had an oil burning "stove-like" heater for warmth at night.

The racks and their accompanying mattresses were well worn and far from comfortable. But at least nobody was in our faces.....and we would only be here for a month. It would do.

We were told where the mess hall was and the

hours it was open. We were told what time to be at morning formation and left to our own devices to get our evening meal and get settled into our living quarters. Being able to take our time eating at the mess hall on our first night as members of the Infantry Training Regiment (ITR) was a luxury almost beyond our comprehension. We actually had time to chew our food, and finish everything on our trays. You could even go back for seconds on something if you wanted to. It felt like we had died and gone to heaven.

The first nights' sleep was fitful at best. There was the lingering excitement of graduating earlier that day, and the anticipation of what our training here would entail. And there was the coldness of our new surroundings. Camp Pendleton is right on the

California coastline, so the wind blowing in off the ocean at night had a real bite to it. Our living area was in a hilly area of the base, so we were at a higher elevation than we had been at the recruit depot, and the area was often blanketed with a cold and damp fog that would roll in during the night and would not burn off until well into the daylight hours. Having grown up in Southern California, I was stunned that it could be so bone chilling cold here.

The oil burning heaters in each Quonset hut were woefully inadequate at heating our living areas. You literally had to stand right next to one in order to feel any heat emanating from it. And it was the month of February, so it wouldn't be warming up any during our stay there......so we just had to adapt to being cold all the time.

We had a company formation every morning at which time one of the troop handlers would read the "orders of the day" out loud to us. They would then tell us what was on the training schedule for that day, after which we would hike to the area where we were to train for that particular day.

At our very first company formation, the troop handler called one private out of the formation and had him stand facing the rest of us. He was of oriental descent, and although certainly not "tiny" in stature, he was rather short compared to most of the other Marines in the company. "This private is a black belt in karate," he told us in a loud voice. "I am appointing him to be my body guard. He will be at my side at all times......except when I send him around to check on things. Whatever he tells you is coming directly from

308

me, so you will do as he tells you. I hope that is clear, because I wouldn't want my body guard to have to hurt anyone!"

It seemed rather odd to some of us that a Marine Corps sergeant would need a body guard, but that turned out to be largely symbolic, just a game the sergeant was playing, at least in everyone's mind except of course the private who had been designated the body guard. He took the role very serious and strutted around the company area in the evening like he owned the joint. He would walk through a hut as though he was a drill instructor, criticizing everyone and everything as he moved about. Most of us just ignored him, but one evening he mouthed off to the wrong private. Private Finnigan was a large burly young man from Boston who was as Irish as a person could be, and had an accent you could cut with a knife. He was also a friend of mine from boot camp and my rack mate here at ITR. It had been a tough training day and it was as cold as a well diggers ass in the hut that night, and Finnigan just couldn't contain himself when the body guard came in and started giving him a hard time.

"Look, asshole," he bellowed at the stunned body guard. "You're just a shit private like the rest of us. You got no business coming in here and talking shit to us. Leave us alone.....go on......get the fuck out of here!"

Everyone in the hut stopped whatever they were doing to watch the action. The body guard was keenly aware that everyone was watching what he would do, and that his reputation as the company bad ass was on the line. The two of them were in a cramped space between the lockers and the racks and there was not much room to move. Doing nothing was not an option for the body guard.......he had been challenged openly and he had to respond. He assumed a fighting stance and let out some sort of guttural scream that I suppose was designed to intimidate Finnigan. But Finnigan not only wasn't intimidated, he seemed to relish the moment.

Finnigan grabbed the smaller man, lifted him off the floor and slammed him into the metal lockers multiple times. It looked like a grizzly bear thrashing around with a rag doll. Then Finnigan stood the body guard up against the lockers and commenced throwing stiff jabs in the body guards' face, so many that it looked like a professional boxer working out on the speed bag, followed by a hard right to his stomach that took the air, and whatever fight was left, right out of the body guard. The body guard curled up in a little ball on the floor and gasped for air, moaning quite loudly. Finnigan stood towering over him until the hapless body guard was finally able to catch his breath. He had no desire for anymore interaction with Finnigan and said weakly "No more."

Finnigan said "Fine.....now get the fuck out of here and don't come back."

The other Marines in the hut buzzed about what they had witnessed well into the night. Of course the general consensus was that Finnigan was in big trouble come daylight. That was Finnigan's opinion as well......he was almost sure there would be brig time involved.

I asked him how he got the best of a black belt karate fighter, and he explained that due to the confined area, he knew the body guard wouldn't have the space he needed to make any effective karate moves. Being the bigger man by far, he just took advantage of the close quarters and literally through his weight around. It also turned out that his father had been a professional boxer and he had grown up around the ring......so he knew how to throw jabs and punches in a very effective manner. Given all the dynamics in play, the body guard had no chance.

At the company formation the next morning, the troop handler looked at the beat up face of his body guard with amazement.

"Body guard.......who did this to you?" he asked.

The body guard cracked a little smile as he responded to the troop handler, obviously thinking that Finnigan would get his now.

"Private Finnigan did this to me, sergeant!" he offered.

"Who is Private Finnigan?" asked the stunned troop handler.

Finnigan slowly raised his hand........expecting something terrible to happen to him.

The troop handler turned to the body guard and said, "Body guard......you're fired! Get back in the ranks."

He then turned to Finnigan and said, "Finnigan......you're the new body guard!"

As Finnigan, and the rest of us would learn

now, the title was strictly honorary. There were no duties assigned to the body guard. The previous body guard had gone around creating havoc strictly on his own......until he got cornered by one cantankerous Irishman twice his size.

During the month we were assigned to the Infantry Training Regiment, we trained hard during the week, but actually got liberty passes on the weekends to leave the base and do as we wished. I took a couple of my buddies home to Riverside a couple of times, where they marveled at getting some home cooked meals and relaxing by my family's swimming pool.

As for the training itself, we hiked too many miles to count as we moved around to the various training ranges on the huge base. We got familiarized with any and all weapons we may have need of in a combat situation. It didn't matter if you were going to be a cook, or a truck driver, or a clerk......you were trained in the use of all weapons. We had left behind the heavier M-14 rifles and were now trained in the use of the newer and much lighter M-16 rifles that were now the weapon of choice in combat. They seemed like they had been manufactured by the Mattel Toy Company to most of us......having lightweight plastic stocks instead of the heavy wood stock we had become accustomed to with the M-14. But we were soon impressed by the amount of firepower these weapons could bring to the party.

We had the opportunity to fire a grenade launcher.....a shoulder held rocket launcher.....an M-60 machine gun......and we threw a live hand grenade. We also went to a night fire range and learned about the effective use of tracer rounds. First, a fire team (four Marines) took a position on the firing line and fired both semi-automatic and then fully automatic rounds at a firing area on the hill across from our position. The tracers lit up the night like the fourth of July and we were amazed at the amount of fire power just four Marines with M-16's could bring to bear. Then a squad took positions and fired........followed by an entire platoon directing fire on the hill across from us. It was hard to imagine that anyone or anything could survive such an onslaught if there had actually been enemy soldiers on that hill. And when an M-60 machine gun opened up on the hill, we fully expected for that poor hill to just disappear under the intensity of the firing. It was truly an impressive display of fire power.

Other highlights included a trip to the gas chamber, where we learned how to properly use a gas mask, what the tear gas felt like when the mask was removed, and how to clear the mask and reapply it after being exposed to the gas. If you ever wanted to see grown men cry, complete with huge streams of snot dangling from their noses......this was the place!

We had some overnight exercises where we ate C-rations and slept on the ground. The C-rations not only contained canned food, crackers and jam, and a chocolate bar.....they also contained a little box with two cigarettes inside. Since I didn't smoke, these made great trading material for someone else's crackers or chocolate bar. There was always someone willing to trade food for smokes.

Throughout our training we kept hearing about Mount Motherfucker, and how we would hate it when we were introduced to it. The day finally came when we hiked most of the day to the location of the infamous Mount Motherfucker. Standing at the bottom of it looking up, it was obvious why it was named as it was......all anyone said as they looked up the mountain we were about to scale, with rifles and full packs in tow, was "mother.........fucker" in an almost reverent tone. Standing there at the bottom, it seemed unlikely that we would be able to scale this thing. But once we were ordered to move out and get our asses to the top......in spite of slipping and sliding at various times, we all helped pull, push, and basically just will each other to the top. Standing on top and looking back down where we had just started

319

our climb, the words "mother…..fucker" seemed just as appropriate as they did when we first arrived.

The month passed quickly and the day finally came when we all prepared to go home on leave prior to reporting to our next duty stations. It was with a certain amount of sadness that I said good bye and good luck to some of the young men I had grown close to during training, as I knew our paths were not likely to cross again. Most of them were headed for Viet Nam, and I was one of the few headed to Memphis……which still stuck in my craw, but I knew there was nothing I could do about it. My buddy Finnigan, however, was one that would be going to Memphis with me…..so I knew at the very least, I would have a body guard there.

As I prepared to leave Camp Pendleton

behind, I reflected on just how far I had come since stepping off that bus back in early October. In just four months' time, I had been transformed from a scared and undisciplined civilian "kid" into a lean, green, fighting machine. I was in the best physical condition of my life and was bursting with self-confidence. I was proud to be wearing the uniform of a United States Marine and looked forward to whatever challenges were to present themselves to me during the course of my enlistment.

Epilog

My career in the Marine Corps covered the span from 1969 to 1979. I had been trained in aviation electronics in Memphis and then served at the Marine Corps Air Station in El Toro, California through July of 1972. At that time, I received orders to the Fleet Marine Corps, Pacific......which meant I would be doing an overseas tour of 13 months. With my specific occupational specialty, I was likely to serve most of that time in Japan at the Marine Corps Air Station in Iwakuni Japan......which I did. Early in 1973, the bulk of forces were removed from Viet Nam, with many of them transported through our air base.....so any chance I had of finally doing some time in the war zone disappeared. I did enjoy working on the flight line and watching my squadron's F-4 Phantoms hit the afterburners and streak off into the sky......and I enjoyed being a Marine, now holding the rank of sergeant. So I re-enlisted for an additional six years while I was still in Japan. While I never made it to Viet Nam, I did have the opportunity to see Okinawa and spent about a month in the Philippine Islands before I returned stateside in August of 1973.

I served a couple of years in a squadron based in Yuma, Arizona and then received orders to attend recruiter's school for assignment to independent duty as a recruiter. Upon completing recruiter's school, I was assigned to recruiting station Chicago, Illinois for the next 39 months.

I performed to the best of my ability while on recruiting duty, but did not enjoy the assignment in

323

the least. I was promoted to Staff Sergeant shortly after reporting to Chicago, and represented my beloved Marine Corps in the best fashion possible. But this was not what I joined the Marine Corps to do. I felt like a caged tiger during the long hours spent in an office environment. I was greatly relieved when my tour was over and I received orders back to my previous squadron in Yuma, Arizona. I felt that once I got re-acclimated to the flight line and working around the Phantom jets again, I could put recruiting duty behind me and would stay a Marine for as long as they would have me. Unfortunately, after just two months back in Yuma, and just two months short of my current enlistment expiring, I was summoned by the commanding officer who informed me that recruiting duty was such a critical assignment at that point in time, that Headquarters Marine Corps had asked him to interview me for a return to recruiting duty. It was clear to me that if I re-enlisted and continued my career as a Marine, I would spend the bulk of that time on recruiting duty......and I was not willing to do that. So I made the decision to allow my enlistment to expire and left the Marine Corps early in 1979.

I went on to have two more distinctively different careers after leaving the Marine Corps, each one challenging and satisfying in its' own way. But I look back to my days spent as a United States Marine as the time in my life when I was truly fulfilled, confident, and extremely proud. I know what an honorable legacy the Marine Corps has in our great country, and I was proud to have been a part of it.

Every success I've had in my adult life can be traced back in some way to the training and experience I received from the Marine Corps. I've heard the saying that "Once a Marine, always a Marine" and I couldn't agree more. I burst with pride every time I see a Marine Corps color guard or the Marine Corps band in action. And I feel as if I have lost a family member each time there is a report of a Marine death somewhere in the world.

Years after leaving the Marine Corps, a replica of the Viet Nam Memorial Monument ("The Wall") came to my city for display. I dug out my platoon book from boot camp and carefully examined the section of wall where they might have been listed if they had fallen in combat. One by one, I looked for each name.......and to my great relief, I found none

326

of them. I tried to remember the names of my fellow

recruits from my first platoon as well, and checked

for their names on the wall as best I could remember.

Of the ones I could remember, I couldn't find their

names on the wall either. This was a great relief to

me, as I knew that many of them had undoubtedly

served in combat, and all had apparently survived the

experience.

So..........God bless Chesty? You bet your

ass! God bless Chesty Puller, and Dan Daly, and

Smedley Butler, and everyone who has ever worn, is

wearing, or will one day wear the uniform of a United

States Marine. There is no better fighting force or

brotherhood anywhere in the world, and our country

owes much to their courage.

Semper Fidelis

Acknowledgements

Since I make reference to three historical figures in this book, Chesty Puller, Smedley Butler, and Dan Daly, I did refer to Wikipedia articles on all three to ensure my recollections of what we were taught about these Marines while in boot camp were accurate.

Pictured is the author G.W. Andrews
with his grandparents and daughter
in May 1975 before leaving to a new
assignment as a Marine recruiter.

Made in United States
North Haven, CT
27 March 2022

17610866R00183